THANK
YOU,
MORE
PLEASE

THANK YOU, MORE PLEASE

a feminist guide to breaking dumb dating rules and finding love

LILY WOMBLE

LEGACY
LIT

New York Boston

Legacy Lit
Hachette Book Group
1290 Avenue of the Americas
New York, NY 10104
LegacyLitBooks.com
@LegacyLitBooks

First Edition: June 2024

Legacy Lit is an imprint of Grand Central Publishing. The Legacy Lit name and logo are registered trademarks of Hachette Book Group, Inc.

The publisher is not responsible for websites (or their content) that are not owned by the publisher.

The Hachette Speakers Bureau provides a wide range of authors for speaking events. To find out more, go to hachettespeakersbureau.com or email HachetteSpeakers@hbgusa .com.

Legacy Lit books may be purchased in bulk for business, educational, or promotional use. For information, please contact your local bookseller or the Hachette Book Group Special Markets Department at special.markets @hbgusa.com.

Print book interior design by Marie Mundaca

Library of Congress Cataloging-in-Publication Data
Names: Womble, Lily, author.
Title: Thank you, more please : a feminist guide to breaking dumb dating rules and finding love / Lily Womble.
Description: First edition. | New York : Legacy Lit, [2024] |
Identifiers: LCCN 2023051331 | ISBN 9781538756843 (hardcover) | ISBN 9781538756867 (ebook)
Subjects: LCSH: Dating (Social customs) | Single women. | Man-woman relationships. | Feminism.
Classification: LCC HQ801 .W797 2024 | DDC 306.73--dc23/eng/20231115
LC record available at https://lccn.loc.gov/2023051331

ISBNs: 978-1-5387-5684-3 (hardcover); 978-1-5387-5686-7 (ebook)

Printed in the United States of America

LSC-H

Printing 1, 2024

To Chris. Thank you for being the reason I know more is possible.

CONTENTS

CONTENTS

INTRODUCTION

Dating Is Way Deeper Than Dating: My Long-Ass Feminist Manifesto

Dating is hard as hell (duh). If you're reading this book, you've probably been in this vicious cycle:

"I want to find someone!"

Then the inevitable, "Woof, it sucks out there. I don't *need* someone. I'm good on my own! No more dating for me!"

And then your best friend gets into a new relationship and you feel a pang of "Ugh, but I really want to find someone. Maybe I should start dating again…"

Cue the ritual of downloading and deleting (and downloading and deleting!) all the dating apps.

Can I get into your brain for a second? Are you consistently asking yourself:

Why am I still single?

Why did it happen for my friends so easily and not for me?

Is there something wrong with me?

And the kicker: *Will I just die alone?*

At the core of all these questions is this truth: You want something. It's not here yet. Your brain is working overtime to try to figure out how to fix that "problem."

You are a brilliant, ambitious, feminist-as-hell human who has created an extraordinary life. How do I know this? Because you're reading this book. I also know you're courageous at work, have amazing friends, care deeply about the well-being of the humans around you, and excel at whatever you put your mind to. So why does your love life feel so different?

Dating is one of the most vulnerable things you can do as a human. It's like wearing your heart outside your body. It's the pang of loneliness you might feel on a solo Saturday while enjoying your gorgeous apartment and wanting someone to share it with. It's the longing to find the right romantic partner to build a family and go snorkeling on three different continents with. It's the desire to find love and the suckyness of dating that can be intense and existentially exhausting. You might try to push away those thoughts and go into overachiever, high-functioning mode to "fix" the problem.

Then your brain tries to figure out your singleness in other ways: You have thoughts like:

Maybe I should lose some weight?

Maybe I'm asking for too much?

Maybe I am too much?

You toy with the idea of hiring a matchmaker. Then after tiring yourself out (and having way too many people tell you, "It happens when you least expect it!"), you stop all active dating and declare to your loved ones, "I'm done. It will happen when I least expect it."

And then you dust off the old dating app again when your last single friend falls in love with someone she met on another dating app. At the core of this hamster wheel is a major flaw (and it's not you):

There has been a massive revolution in the way women have been taught to achieve over the past fifty years. There are so many books about how to negotiate for raises or how to assert your value in the workplace.

But the way we have been taught to date is still stuck in the dark ages.

We've been taught that we should trust an app to deliver us from singleness. We've been told that wanting a relationship too badly is "desperate." That desire for the right partner (and the feeling of *What's wrong with me that I haven't found someone?*) makes you less of a powerful badass. There's also a dirty myth floating around popular consciousness that wanting a partner makes you less feminist.

Then, in the opposite direction, there's the very real social construct that women are looked upon as "less valuable" if they don't have a romantic partner.

In response, conventional dating wisdom says: if you want to find love, don't trust yourself. This can sound like the following:

> "Are you sure you know what you want?"
>
> "Play the numbers game! Let me swipe for you!"
>
> "Maybe you should try this new dating app I read about!"
>
> "Are you being too picky?"
>
> "Maybe you should just go on more dates."

This kind of advice equals exhausting yourself with dates, dating like it's your part-time job, and lowering your standards because "you never know who is right for you, right?"

I would hear this all the time from my friends and family when I was single and really struggling to find the right connection (or really *any* connection). Then, after years working in the dating industry as a professional matchmaker and then dating coach, I saw this old-fashioned dating advice for what it was: harmful and sexist.

These norms are the reason I ended up in the worst romantic relationship of my life. And they're probably part of the reason you feel miserable in your dating life too. Right now, those shitty norms are embedded in most dating advice, dating services, and dating support.

INTRODUCING: THE PATRIARCHY

The patriarchy is a leading force in why dating feels so dang hard and arduous, for everyone, and especially for women. The patriarchy is a very prominent character in this book, so let's get to know it a bit, shall we?

The patriarchy is one of the main reasons dating feels so draining and treacherous. The patriarchy is a central villain in this book, and to catch you up, here's the definition from the *Cambridge English Dictionary*:

> *Patriarchy*: Control by men, rather than women or both men and women, of most of the power and authority within a society.

What other fucked-up system predated and created the patriarchy? White supremacy. These systems of oppression are embedded in our society to keep power with people who are primarily cisgender-male, wealthy, straight, able-bodied, and white.

This is why I call myself an "intersectional feminist" dating coach. Because if dating matters to our personal well-being, I believe the inverse is also true—the way we find love, the way I coach, and the way we do life matters to the well-being of others around us.

Intersectional feminism is another main character in this book, so let's give it a little more context:

As *Merriam Webster's* defines it, feminism is the "belief in and advocacy of the political, economic, and social equality of the sexes."

"Feminist" also is a "dirty word" to those invested in upholding the status quo and those who have learned to survive by maintaining it.

Intersectional feminism, a term coined by Kimberlé Crenshaw, an American civil rights advocate and a leading scholar of critical race theory, is "a prism for seeing the way in which various forms of inequality often operate together and exacerbate each other."

I don't think we can talk about creating a badass dating life for you (and millions of readers around the world) in a meaningful way without talking about the dating industry (and the dating process) being a hotbed for harmful patriarchal norms. These norms tell women to shrink themselves to be more "appeasing." These norms also foster the racism, homophobia, and transphobia that run rampant in the dating landscape today.

And for full disclosure, as you can probably tell from my *iconic* author photo on the book, I'm a white woman. I also am cisgender, bisexual, and married to a cisgender man in a straight-presenting relationship. I carry a ton of unearned privilege in this world. There are things that I will mess up in this book, things I'll get wrong, and things that will change with time. I know that I'm an imperfect human writing an imperfect book. I also know that as this advice and these tools have supported hundreds before you, they will support you in creating the love life you want too.

I'm here writing this book through this intersectional feminist lens because there is major work to do—in dating and everywhere else.

As Audre Lorde said, "I am not free while any woman is unfree, even when her shackles are very different from my own."

Here's another way this intersectional feminist lens impacts our work together: I know that you are whole right now, with or without a relationship. You get to find what you want with *all* your badass ambition, power, and confidence.

My mission is to help you create *your own* path through the potentially treacherous dating waters. One that prioritizes your self-care, your boundaries, and your complete worthiness. Outside of the status quo is a dating life that is more joyful and more vibrant than you can imagine right now (thank you, more please!).

For those in the back saying, "Huh? What does all this feminist stuff have to do with my dating life? Are you saying all men are bad and that I have to consider myself a feminist to find love?"

First of all, being a feminist for me is about the liberation of all people. I believe feminism is a tool for collective as well as personal freedom, and in your dating life, it's a tool to fight and release norms that are keeping you and your needs shoved into a box.

Believing that not all men are terrible and seeing the need for major change are truths that can both exist at once. It's called "both/and," and you're going to hear a lot of "both/and" statements and ideas in this book.

So why do I think the patriarchy is (mostly) responsible for dating feeling horrible?

If the patriarchy is interested in keeping power in the hands of the powerful, then it's in its best interest for women to settle.

So our society actively socializes women to not trust themselves. Women are taught to be "nice" at the expense of being bold and honest. We teach women that they are "selfish" for wanting what they want or being ambitious, fierce, and complex.

We learn that to be single is to be less than, and because we as humans are neurobiologically wired to desire belonging (and hardwired to fear rejection like death!), the societally acceptable alternative is to settle down with a nice-enough cisgender man to make babies and produce more labor for the workforce.

Old-fashioned and patriarchal dating standards are only exacerbated by a profit-hungry, addictive (dating apps were literally built like slot machines), three-billion-dollar dating industry. This patriarchal standard might also be perpetuated (on purpose or by default) by friends and family who were taught how to survive by making themselves and their needs smaller. That was the case for me.

From an early age, I was sensitive, creative, opinionated, and leading every club. For example, in first grade, I was excluded from the other girls' fairy game at recess. They didn't want to play with me, so I made that mean something was wrong with me. I responded by doing what I was born to do: boss people around (in other words, lead).

So I started a recycling club. I founded an organization, organized a class-wide cleanup of the playground, and successfully lobbied to get the first recycling can by the principal's office of my elementary school. I was very proud. My mom still has the hand-drawn brochure I made for the Helping Hands Club, and she framed the picture of me shaking my principal's hand at the unveiling ceremony.

When I was twelve, my mom, who is a gorgeous, creative, talented-as-hell human, was usually very encouraging of my leading, recycling habits, singing, and general "Lilyness."

But one day, when we were talking about my future, boys, and dating, she looked at me and said, "Lily, you're too much for most people. You're going to have a hard time finding a husband who can handle you."

Her words cut immediately. Especially considering how much I loved playing dress-up in my mom's beautiful wedding dress. Were the kids in class right? Was I "too much" to be wanted by anyone for the rest of my life? Would I not get to wear a wedding dress of my own? Was that only meant for girls who weren't "too much," like me?

Then confusion set in. My brain was trying to work out the calculus of why my mom told me this so young. Was I so broken that I needed to be prepared from *this* age for my love life to be terrible? (I found out later that she was told this when she was twelve by her older brother. Hello, generational, patriarchal trauma.)

I also knew intuitively that "having a hard time finding a husband" was a big deal.

I was raised in Alabama, where I saw that a woman's worth was tied solely to her relationship status with a cisgender man. In this context, marriage meant safety, belonging, and literally survival.

I went to wedding after wedding, where the bride said, in her freaking *vows*, "I promise to be subservient to my husband."

And for the man: "I promise to lead my wife like Christ led the church."

Even at age twelve, this pissed me off. This, paired with my mom's words about my "too muchness," felt like a life sentence of loneliness. My brain was a noodle soup of confusing contradictions, such as, "You don't want to be subservient, but you're also too much. That is why no one wants to be your friend, and this all disqualifies you from most people. Good luck out there, ya old maid."

I was thinking this at age twelve.

After I was indoctrinated into the "you're too much" belief, I went out in the world with this mission to be a fierce, independent feminist—*and* to prove my mom wrong, a truly pressure-packed recipe doomed from the start.

Cut to my mid-twenties. I hadn't been in a relationship since high school, I hadn't had sex yet, and I felt light-years behind my peers.

When I was twenty-one, trying to shed the "late bloomer" identity, I cut up my Alabama-government-sanctioned abstinence pledge (which was in the form of a hard square of plastic resembling a credit card that I was forced to sign in seventh grade in front of my frumpy gym coach). Side note: it lived in my wallet unironically for a decade until I'd grown out of this phase. I could now proclaim that I was *ready to get it on*. My burgeoning sexuality meant all possibilities of hookups felt *electric*.

But after a few significant make-out sessions and hard encounters with men who pressured me for more than I was ready for, I found that casual sex was decidedly not my thing. This was yet another way I felt weird and "behind."

In my professional life, I'd just moved to New York City after burning out from a career in feminist advocacy work. For years I'd been working for organizations fighting for women's reproductive rights in Mississippi, attending conferences on the global status of women's rights in Turkey, and even speaking at a women's reproductive rights conference in Malaysia.

The well-being of women and girls has always been at the center of my heart and purpose. After growing up in Birmingham, Alabama, my righteous anger toward the patriarchal status quo was my love language.

At the same time, I was always furiously searching for my husband in every grocery store, at every job interview, and during every late-night shift. In my brain was always the ambient hum of: *You are too much* and *not enough. You have to prove that story wrong! You have to find a relationship or that means you're literally doomed for all eternity to singleness and less-than-wholeness.*

I was swiping for dates online a bunch at work. At the time, I had four survival jobs: preschool teacher, babysitter, receptionist, and, most iconically, balloon-hat maker at Señor Frog's Times Square.

I would wear my best form-fitting tee and jeans and walk around with my I TWIST FOR TIPS pin on my shirt. I would hold a giant barrel of blown-up balloons above my head, asking table by table who wanted a Viking/flower/monkey-in-a-palm-tree hat. And after 10 p.m., I'd ask, "Who wants a penis balloon hat?" I could also make a dick cumming into a pair of lips as a *hat*. I was *really* talented.

I made all-cash tips and no hourly wage. I remember going to the Bank of America ATM at 1 a.m. depositing my one-dollar bills one at a time for an hour. I couldn't do it all at once because those bills were in such tattered shape and I wanted every single one to count.

I was making pretty good money for a balloon-hat twister. But I was also having pretty bad panic attacks in the back on my breaks. I struggled with anxiety, and the strobe lights, coupled with having to yell over the remixed Jason Derulo to ask for tips, was not my vibe.

One slow Saturday 4 p.m. shift at Señor Frog's, I was swiping on a dating app and came across a profile that caught my eye. I thought, *Huh, OK. He went to a great graduate school, so he's smart. Cute enough. Kind of witty in his profile.* Swipe right.

We started chatting. He asked me to go out that night. I was hesitant, but my coworkers talked me into going.

I got there twenty minutes early and made friends with the bartender. My date walked in looking disheveled. After a bit of awkward conversation, I shot a knowing glance toward the bartender that said, "This won't last long."

My date shared that he was just in New York for the summer and he lived somewhere else for his degree. So this guy was just here for two months. Interesting.

We drank too much red wine, and as alcohol will do, it lubed up the conversation and the connection. A few glasses each later, I asked him back to my place. At the time, I was living in a dorm room at a progressive Christian church in the middle of Midtown

Manhattan, where I was working at their nonprofit in exchange for rent. *Iconic!*

It was a fun rompy night. We had brunch together the next day. Suddenly, it felt like something serious immediately. *Sex. Brunch. Was this it?!*

This new man, Dylan, and I became exclusive within two weeks. I was turned on by his intellect; he was turned on by my sparkly personality. We said "I love you" very quickly. We had sex. I'd lost my virginity and was smitten.

I couldn't believe that someone would want to be with me. After feeling lonely and "too much" for most of my life, especially to men, I felt like a runner in the Marathon des Sables—which is literally a 156-mile, six-day marathon in the Sahara.

I had been running for so long in the heat and was searching for water and a cool place to lay my head. This new relationship quenched that thirst.

The thing about the Sahara, though, is that what feels luxurious may just be the bare minimum.

Having a boyfriend felt like telling the world that I was OK. I was lovable. I was chosen. Everyone (in my head) could stop freaking out about whether or not I was "too much" to find someone. *See?* There is someone right here who is proving to *everyone* (again, only me in my head) that I'm not too much to have love.

I couldn't wait for my friends and family to hear the news. There would be no more Lily complaining about her dating life and wondering if it would ever happen for her. You can move on with your worries because she's been *chosen* by a *man*, y'all! I couldn't wait to show off this new relationship and to have a plus one to kiss on a bridge somewhere.

That summer, my good friend was getting married in Amsterdam. Two months into dating, in a flurry of boldness, I asked Dylan to go to Europe with me to this wedding. He said yes.

My brain was in a tizzy and began thinking, *OMG! He's coming to Europe with me. This is serious. Is this the whirlwind romance I've been reading about in books? Could this be it?*

A few days later, he said he wanted to come to Europe with me, just not to the wedding with my friends. He said that we weren't serious enough for him to be a date to my friend's wedding. (Red Flag Alert!)

Well, I thought, *compromise is important in relationships (or so I've heard). He has his reasons and he still wants to be with me, so that's what matters. Maybe it is too early for him to meet my friends.*

To prepare for the trip (which I very much could not afford), I excitedly got my first credit card, paid for my flights and Airbnbs, and got on a plane solo to the wedding. I had a blast, and then a few days later, I met up with my boyfriend for one night in Amsterdam; then it was off to Paris. Hello, dream trip!

We stayed in this little flat on the top floor of a quintessential Parisian apartment building. It was so romantic and…intimate. The tiny studio didn't have its own toilet. The shower was in the bedroom. Pooping became a whole to-do involving several flights of stairs, and peeing became exclusively a task handled in the shower.

Dylan and I were peeing in front of each other in this tiny

studio apartment. This relationship was very serious. *I was living the freaking dream.*

We went to dinner our first night and ordered some wine and chicken, and I could tell something was off. He became really quiet and distant, and halfway through the meal he looked at me and said, "Lily, I need to tell you something."

"Yeah, what's up?"

"This isn't working for me. I can't do this anymore. I know we said we were monogamous, but I can't be in an exclusive relationship. I need an open relationship or we can't be together."

Fear rushed through my body.

This was my first adult relationship, my first time having sex with someone, and my first time being intimate with someone I loved.

The facade was cracked. This felt completely out of the blue. We'd decided on being monogamous, I was finally *not* "too much," and he, on our first night in Paris, had to drop (what felt like) a bomb.

Look, to the nonmonogamous and nonmonog-curious reader, I get that open relationships work for so many humans. I do not believe that monogamy is the gold standard of human romantic relationships. *Both/and* it's what I wanted and what we'd decided on, together.

The way he was explaining it, I felt like a dummy for having that preference. He talked at me about the benefits of nonmonogamy. The higher quality of communication it took. The fact that he lost interest in romantic partners after a while and this was a way for him to keep our amazing relationship going and get his needs met.

But all I heard was, "You're too much. I don't want to be with just you."

In my fantasy now, I stand up, thank him for the good times, leave the table, and have a glorious solo trip in Paris. Instead, I shrank. This felt like my only hope at a romantic partnership, after years of dry, lonely desert sand.

I decided to try it. I thought that it was *selfish* to want the kind of relationship I was yearning for. I also didn't think that more was out there for me.

The tape in my head was playing:

You can't always get what you want.

This is it. You have to compromise, remember? That's what relationships are. You're too much for most people.

And underneath all of it was the drumbeat of scarcity: *You probably won't find anyone else.*

It also felt like choosing to be single after *finally* finding someone who wanted to be with me would be stupid and selfish.

Coming back to you and me, reader. Let's check out what was going on here, underneath the surface:

I was holding an internalized belief that I was "too much." This was a well-trodden neural pathway in my mind that was established with heavy patriarchal socialization, parental confirmation, and social proof (e.g., I felt lonely most of the time). This belief didn't feel like a choice. It *was* my state of being.

I was trying to unbelieve that story by taking action.

I was searching for love with the primary goal of proving that "too much" story wrong. What I didn't realize was that in doing so, I was centering that "I'm too much" story as the truth of who I was. I put the power of slaying that dragon in the hands of a man.

Unknowingly, I had done exactly that which I most despised (and that which is also very natural survival behavior): **I became subservient to the patriarchy in order to belong.**

That's the other bit that's so incredibly frustrating about dating: It might feel like your love life success is in the hands of someone else. That one day, it will just randomly happen, when someone turns around, sees you afresh, and chooses you. Essentially this fantasy points to the belief that you are totally out of control.

This idea that the partnership I craved was completely out of my hands and that "when a romantic partner chooses you, you're more whole and valuable" felt unavoidable and true for me.

If this hits home for you right now, know that you're not alone. This book is about offering a different path forward. One that prioritizes your desires, your wholeness, and your agency. You have more power here than you think, and this path leads to finding extraordinary partnership, on your terms. We're going to move through this, together.

Now, back to the bleakness.

I was now talking myself into an open relationship with the first adult love I'd ever had. I was holding on to a very unappealing either/or decision in my head. Either you get into this box and keep having a boyfriend who you also confusingly are still in love with *or* you choose not to be in this relationship.

This kind of settling felt like survival. In a historical context, settling for less than what we want makes complete sense.

Human brains are making meaning and telling stories from the data around us all the time to keep us safe. In our recent collective memory, we've fought with the reality that:

> Women couldn't get a credit card without their *husband's permission* until 1974.
>
> Same-sex marriage wasn't legalized in the United States until 2015.
>
> People with uteruses do not have rights over their reproductive choices in most of the United States as of 2024.

In this context, why the hell would we feel like we had absolute agency over our romantic choices?

So of course we gaslight ourselves into bad-news relationships to escape the constant fear of what it means about us if we "die alone."

Of course we, as badass feminist humans, buck against this internalized patriarchal narrative and then swing to the opposite end of hyperindependence and declare, "I don't need anyone!" Only to deprive ourselves of the very real and tender desire for a soul-affirming romantic partner.

I was trying to "high-achiever" my way through this predicament. I did a bunch of research on different forms of nonmonogamy, and I made a list of all the expectations and questions I had in this open relationship arrangement (e.g., Are we primary partners? What do we share and when? How often are we going to talk?). I scheduled a formal sit-down to discuss these things with him. I thought it would help us both get our needs met.

It felt empowering to dive deep and take part in this decision-making. Though looking back, I was actually researching how to dress a wound after the trauma had already happened. I just wanted to slap a Band-Aid on there and get going with this relationship.

Dylan said that he loved me and that he wanted to meet my needs. I would find out later that what he really wanted was the benefits of dating me without any of the emotional support or true partnership. I would ask for what I wanted, and his response was "I think that's doable! I love you! I want to meet your needs!"

After months of flakiness with dates, blaming me for wanting "too much" communication, hesitancy to meet my loved ones, and hot-and-cold affection, his actions clearly communicated, "Your needs are too much."

Cue me crying on my bedroom floor, internalizing what I might have done wrong. This person clearly stated that he could not meet my needs. Because I wanted this so desperately to work, I gaslit myself into believing this was normal. Relationships sometimes feel miserable, right? Relationships take work, right? No one person can meet all your needs, right?

At the same time as this relationship was getting more and more toxic for me, I was looking for yet another survival job in NYC. (Señor Frog's went out of business in Times Square; RIP. My balloon-twisting talent would now be unused.)

My friend was side hustling with this matchmaking firm, let's call it HitchHub. She encouraged me to apply. I didn't really want to. I ended up submitting an application thinking that it would be a funny story one day of how I applied to be a matchmaker.

My emotional intelligence skills (with other people) were off the charts. I could do some incredible empathetic reflective listening in a conversation. I'd had years of practice bartering vulnerability and caregiving for connection. This was a snap for me.

I skated through the interview process and moved through their wild role-playing scenarios. For example, I was given the following circumstance: "You just set up a date between a man and a woman (your client). She is sitting at the bar, and the man walks in, takes one look at her, and then leaves. You have to have a call with your client to explain what happened and you don't want her to ask for a refund. *Go!*" (This actually *did* happen, btw.)

I got the job and took on my first client. I remember Dylan being in my room when I was searching the matchmaking database for her. He asked, "What do you think is wrong with these women that they'd pay tens of thousands for a service they can just do themselves?"

I responded, "Dating is fucking hard. They want hope. They want support. Maybe I can give that to them."

As I was actively making myself and my needs smaller in this relationship, I was also *professionally* setting up dates and getting really good at it (I became the third most "successful" matchmaker out of 160 in the U.S., cue hair flip). I was telling my clients they deserved more than their past terrible relationships. I was swiping on all the dating apps for them and urging them not to settle for less.

There was a Grand Canyon–level disconnect. Here I was

taking all the scraps I was accepting here on Earth, and there was the advice I was giving all the way over there on Mars.

As a professional matchmaker and a very single woman for most of my life, I was petrified of what it would mean about me if I was single again. I was afraid that what I wanted didn't exist. I was afraid that I wanted "too much" and that I was "too much" for true love and belonging.

The loneliness I was feeling before this terrible relationship was worse than the anxiety attacks. The pressure was on. My identity as a feminist, as a woman, and as a human who wanted belonging felt like it was on the line.

Matchmaking while I was in this terrible relationship taught me a core lesson:

Dating is way deeper than dating.

How we find love, the kind of love we accept—it is a personal and political act. The way we do one thing is the way we do everything.

This is why I call dating a microcosm of every hope, dream, fear, insecurity, and desire that you have as a human. It matters to your well-being. How you date can also create waves of change in your life, as well as in the world around you.

Thank You, More Please is going to guide you, step-by-step, through audaciously asking for and receiving more in your love life than ever before. Which means rewriting your old dating-life beliefs that helped you survive (and that are no longer serving you), unpacking your past relationship patterns with intention, redefining your preferences on an essence-based level, and creating an authentic dating strategy to attract the partnership you desire. It's a "Thank you" to all your brilliance and a big "More please" to everything you desire. All of this work is going to help you create a confident and joyful-as-fuck dating life that makes the right relationship inevitable. And it's exactly how I eventually attracted the love of my life.

This work is exactly what got me (and hundreds of women around the world) from toxic, crying on-the-bedroom-floor relationships, from crippling self-doubt and loneliness, into the most self-trusting, agency-filled lives imaginable. Attracting extraordinary love then becomes the bonus.

So let's break all the dumb dating rules, celebrate exactly who you are right now (thank you!), and create your most epic love life, one that attracts more than you thought possible (more please!).

THANK YOU, MORE PLEASE

1

It's Time for a Dating Detox

To get the love life you want, you've got to stop dating.

So I challenge you to go on a Dating Detox for at least a month.

That means put a pause on all active dating, delete all your dating apps, and stop obsessing over how to "fix your dating life." I dare you.

You might read that and think, *Whew, I'm so glad someone's given me permission to stop trying because this shit is exhausting.*

Or you might think, *Active dating?! What's that? I haven't found a good date in years.*

Or your brain might be telling you, *Ugh, Lily, I want to find someone. Give me the sauce already!*

If you had any of these thoughts, welcome to the last Dating Detox you'll ever need.

Remember in the introduction where I said dating apps are like slot machines that are designed to addict us and leave us a messy blob of anxious dating efforts?

NOW INTRODUCING: THE DATING CASINO

I've seen *Ocean's Eleven* more than fifty times, so I consider myself a casino expert. If you haven't seen this 2001 classic film, George Clooney, aka Danny Ocean, is leading ten other guys (no women star in the film except for Julia Roberts, who is a stunning damsel in distress) in robbing three casinos in one epic night. To prepare, Danny Ocean has everyone on the team do reconnaissance to learn as much about their target as possible. He describes the casino business like this—"They were built as labyrinths to keep people in." All the winding lanes, the flashing lights, and the exits being impossible to find, it's how they make all that money.

The same is true for the dating world and how it keeps us all stuck.

The Dating Casino is full of everything you've done to find love over the years. Every slot machine and every blackjack table includes every piece of dating advice, everything you've ever tried to meet your person, every rejection and relationship that didn't work, and every hopeful date that went south. You were taught to gather your coins, put on your best outfit, and come to the table again and again to hopefully hit the jackpot (i.e., find the relationship of your dreams, make your way to the Elvis Wedding Chapel, get hitched, and live happily ever after).

Inside the Dating Casino, the dating apps are the bright,

shiny slot machines that are dinging at you all the time. They are enticing you to come spend your quarters in a hurry because the triple cherry is just one pull away. The apps lure you in by telling you that love is just "one swipe away." After trying over and over again, you numb out by mindlessly pulling the lever. Or you burn out from the endless dates (the constant *ping ping ping ping ping*—there are more pings, but I'm annoyed just writing this) and you walk away.

Suddenly, your friend yells out, "OMG! I just landed a jackpot! I'm getting married tomorrow. Just go around and play a bunch of games!" You take her advice, fill yourself up with more hope, and play a shit ton of games, but nothing happens. In fact, you end up losing more time, sanity, and money (dating is dang expensive). You find yourself thinking, *Am I doing this wrong? How did this work for her and not me?*

So then you commiserate with the other "losers" in the Dating Casino who haven't won or even gotten close in years. This is when you go out with other single friends and get stuck in a loop of conversation about how hard dating is, bemoan how men, women, people in general, suck, and declare that there are "no good prospects out there!" Around and around you go, and then your mom sets you up with her neighbor's dentist, who is "such a catch," and you think, *Nothing else has worked, so I might as well try this.* But then he drones on and on about cavities and you realize he hasn't brushed his hair in what looks like a decade.

You feel overwhelmed and stuck. Where should you go? Should you stop trying? Why has this worked for other people and not for you? Your brain is fried. You're hungry. It's lonely in the

Dating Casino, as seemingly you're the only person who hasn't hit it big. You were told that to win, you had to play the games *exactly* right, but it led nowhere. It looks like other people win, just not you.

Are you with me in this long-ass analogy? You might be wondering, *Why is dating this dang hard?*

Inside the Dating Casino, there's also a lot of stuff that people don't tell you about. There's the settling for a relationship that is just "good enough," the intense emotional labor of scanning every room you're in vigilantly for any single person who exists, or the toxic-positivity push to "just be more confident" so you can land a partner (without any follow-up explaining *how* to build that confidence).

And underneath all this is the constant pressure of living within the patriarchy.

The patriarchy is one of the main reasons dating feels so exhausting and treacherous. In a 2018 *Guardian* article entitled "The Age of Patriarchy: How an Unfashionable Idea Became a Rallying Cry for Feminism Today," Charlotte Higgins unpacks the historical context of the word "patriarchy" and offers another helpful, modern definition: "At its simplest, [patriarchy] conveys the existence of a societal structure of male supremacy that operates at the expense of women—rather in the way that 'white supremacy' conveys the existence of a societal structure that operates at the expense of Black people."

As a reminder from the introduction, we're taking an intersectional approach to this conversation (because it's always more complex than just one "thing"), so in reference to the patriarchy in this book, know that we're also talking about the systems that created it—aka white supremacy—and the oppressive systems that uphold it—aka capitalism, homophobia, transphobia, and ableism. These are all embedded in American society to keep power with the cis-male, wealthy, straight, able-bodied, and white.

What does this have to do with your dating life? If the patriarchy is looking to uphold the male-dominant status quo, then of course you were socialized to shrink. Shrink your desires, your boundaries, and your opinions, especially in a romantic context. And of course, our patriarchal society has organized itself around an institution that has dominated women for centuries: marriage.

Let's get one thing out in the open: I don't think men are the enemy. I know that men are negatively impacted by patriarchal conditioning as well (we all have a lot to unpack in therapy). As Higgins writes, "'Patriarchy' accommodates the idea that not all men enthusiastically uphold it or benefit equally from it; and that some women may, on the other hand, do a great deal toward supporting it. It also allows for the fact that however much we might loathe it, we all, perforce, participate in it."

I don't think marriage has to be an inherently dominating force. I chose and am married to an incredible man. We cocreate our relationship every single day and unpack our gender roles in couples therapy sometimes weekly. Once you see it, this patriarchy shit takes time to unwind from our lives and relationships, no matter what identities you hold.

The problem here is that this cocktail of patriarchy and centuries of power has created a culture in which women are made to feel like losers if they haven't landed in a romantic relationship.

Women are made to feel like something *must* be wrong if a man hasn't *chosen* you!

This toxic message is sometimes loud. It comes down on you hard at the holidays when your mom gives you the shitty, twin-size, blow-up mattress on the floor in the living room right next to your three nieces and nephews. Meanwhile she gives your childhood bedroom to your sister and her partner. (In other words, "Single women must make themselves uncomfortable on vacations and be the de facto caregiver because they are not yet partnered.")

Sometimes the message is stealthier—such as when your boss passes you over for a huge opportunity at work. He and his wife have been socializing with your coworker and his wife at company parties. And you, the single one, aren't invited to couples-bonding activities.

This can also be more quietly inferred by your coupled friends who don't invite you to stuff anymore because you're not in a relationship.

It's the impulse to stay with someone who is wrong for you because of your fear that no one else will want to be with you.

The patriarchy can also manifest as an ex who gaslit you into believing you were crazy for wanting more.

It's a "dating expert" who tells you that *you* are the problem for being too picky and for not being feminine enough.

Some of these ideas and this feedback may be well intentioned, but the impact on single women is existential exhaustion. It's hard to get a deep breath in this dating atmosphere that is thick with patriarchal bullshit.

Because the patriarchy has been designed to keep power in

the hands of the already powerful, women have been taught, implicitly and explicitly, that it is selfish to want and directly ask for what we want because it upsets the existing order. If it's selfish to want what you want, then a punishing, miserable dating process only seems logical.

Then there's also a story wafting around in feminist circles that sounds like, "You're less of a feminist if you want a romantic relationship." So either I want a romantic relationship and that makes me basic and less of a feminist *or* I deny my desire for a romantic relationship and remain the strong, independent woman I know I am. The amount of cognitive dissonance I faced as a feminist single woman was exhausting.

All this dating toxicity made me literally sick.

For years, instead of trying to get to the root of the issue, I just kept going on dates, slapped on the thickest foundation I could find, put on the sparkliest nail colors, and kept playing in the Dating Casino. But my dating problems got worse. By my mid-twenties, I knew things were bad when I found myself hiding and crying in my then boyfriend's bathroom.

As I shared in the introduction, my ex-boyfriend Dylan and I met on a dating app. He was my first adult relationship, we agreed to being exclusive quickly, and we fell in love—fast. Like, saying "I love you" two weeks in. We went on a vacation to Paris in month two of our relationship (a trip that took me *years* to pay off).

Dylan agreed to come to Paris with me, but *not* to attend my friend's wedding (Eek! Red Flag!). So one evening we were dining at the most idyllic, romantic café on the Seine, and he said, "I either need to be in an open relationship or we need to break up."

Even though I had no interest in nonmonogamy, even though my body was screaming, "This isn't the right thing for you," I chose the former. Staying with Dylan under this new open agreement was a choice that felt necessary. I was afraid that this was it. I was a late bloomer in my mid-twenties who had just had sex for the first time and with this person. I'd never been in an adult romantic relationship, and I thought that meant something about me and my ability to be in a relationship at all.

This choice to be in an open relationship, and then Dylan's subsequent lack of communication and gaslighting when he told me I was wanting "too much," made me physically feel like a discarded, crumpled piece of paper. I thought relationships required this amount of striving and compromise after seeing divorce all around me (including my parents at this time). And I was afraid being single again would mean that I was indeed "too much," and ultimately unworthy of partnership.

After a few months of crying on the phone, no-show dates, and being told my needs were "too much," it turned out Dylan wanted less of an "open relationship" and more of a "nonexistent relationship." I responded by making myself and my needs smaller to appease his capacity. At the time, this choice felt safer than being single.

So, nine months into this "open" relationship, after I sat on his toilet, crying, I looked around his apartment with tears streaming down my face. Then I realized for the first time how filthy his place was. Cat litter all over the floor. Dust and dirty dishes everywhere. It was a lightning-bolt realization that I needed to get out. I realized that I'd been in such survival mode in my love life that

I hadn't acknowledged the chaos that was around me. I had to ask myself, *How the fuck did I end up here?*

"LAUGH OR GET DUMPED"

Before my first date when I was sixteen, I called my aunt, who was my hype woman when it came to all things "becoming a woman." For example, she shaved my armpits for the first time ever with such a ceremony that it became picture-worthy. In the photo, my other aunts and my mom are surrounding us, eagerly looking in for the moment that the Venus razor would validate my status as a woman. I felt equal parts devastatingly embarrassed and excited to be the center of attention and ritual.

My first date would take place at Momma Goldberg's Deli in downtown Homewood. This was an iconic venue for my first-ever foray into romance. Though this restaurant was right beside my favorite coffee shop, I'd never been. It seemed like the place where cool kids with cash to burn who made fun of me at lunchtime would hang out after school. I remember planning my sandwich order the day before. Keeping it simple. A turkey club, hold the mayo.

I called my aunt to hype me up before this date, and of course the whole extended family was with her. The phone got passed to my cousin Kirsten. This moment is burned into my brain and into my love-life timeline. She said with complete seriousness, "Lily, remember to be jovial. Boys like girls who are jovial."

I enthusiastically agreed and decided that I would be Julia Roberts–level laughing and delighted by everything my date said.

What I realized years later is that Cousin Kirsten's advice was code for "Whatever you do, be pleasing to the man in front of you. It makes you more attractive. Laugh—or get dumped." This became a pattern of people-pleasing to get men to stick around in my love life.

I also internalized messages from friends, family, my church youth group interns, and *Seventeen* magazine, like, "It happens when you least expect it, so stop being so desperate." "Go on more dates; it's all a numbers game." "Be sure to give dates one more chance than you want to, you never know!" "Be sure to look your best on dates, which might mean you losing ten pounds—here's how!"

After years of carrying this and more bad advice into adulthood, I became bone-tired of obsessing about whether or not "I was doing it right." Obsessing over whether or not my body was thin enough or my personality palatable enough. These emotional fluctuations led to some major metaphorical bloating. I just wanted relief, so I chose a shitty relationship with Dylan.

When I stopped to look around my dating life on Dylan's toilet, I realized I had a stomachache from all the bullshit I'd ingested from a patriarchal culture that taught me to be more "nice and accommodating" in an effort to catch a dick. My nervous system was fried from the constant anxiety from feeling "behind" and asking myself, *Why is it so easy for them and not for me?*

I needed to purge this dating toxicity.

I needed to stop playing the games I was taught and detox all the dating bullshit that had accumulated over the years. That meant after getting weeks of pep talks from my therapist, I broke up with Dylan. I needed to figure out what dating was going to look like on *my* terms.

This meant detoxing from other people's dating advice that no longer fit me or my values. Detoxing from dating apps. Detoxing from the idea that I had to be "actively dating" to find someone. Detoxing from the scarcity and hustle mindset that kept me inside the rat race of dating.

I had been so busy trying to prove that I was enough by being in a relationship that I hadn't heard the call coming from inside the house: I didn't need a relationship to prove anything about myself. And I get to want a relationship that actually serves me when it comes around. The result of this breakthrough and my own Dating Detox was life-changing.

As Tricia Hersey says in her book, *Rest Is Resistance: A Manifesto*, "Hustle culture is violence." It's time to detox from the idea that you must hustle to find love and from believing that dating has to be punishing and sucky.

Here are the hard, cold facts: The dating industry actually *profits* from you feeling *miserable*. When your brain is addicted to a dating app (as they were built to keep users searching for the next best thing), the dating industry makes money from you mindlessly swiping left and right, being numbed out and exhausted. How? More time on the app means more ads being served to users and more paid app upgrades being purchased. For example, dating apps regularly put basic preference filters behind a paywall, like age and location, making it completely frustrating (and a waste of time) to swipe without upgrading to a five-plus-dollars-per-month plan.

So what the dating industry doesn't want you to know is that there is a more joyful, ease-filled, and self-trusting path forward to finding love. This pathway is completely outside of the hustle and grind of the Dating Casino.

I invite you to follow the stealthily hidden Exit signs in the Dating Casino labyrinth. Once you step outside, you will see a beautiful black SUV waiting for you to enter the Dating Detox Spa. It's the kind of place where you are completely cared for, every need is met, and everything fed to you is healthy and delicious.

When you are ready to set out on this path, you will find love that is so much more beautiful than what the patriarchy has required. This Dating Detox is going to feel *ah-mazing* once you're done, and you'll be ready to take on your dating life in a powerful, superwoman way.

However, I'm going to forewarn you that the Dating Detox Spa won't always be fun. There will be days when you feel like you're at a retreat from hell, where loneliness feels like 6 a.m. hikes and there's no boost of endorphins from a random match. A detox can feel uncomfortable and deeply wrong if you've learned that external action is required to find love. But in order for you, your brain, your body, your self-trust, and your agency to land in the best relationship of your life, you will need to strip away what you've been taught.

> **You have to strip away the hustle, the external noise of bad dating advice, and the constant pressure to move forward.**

The thing about the Dating Detox is that magical, weird, awesome shit happens when you cut out the dating noise and start listening to your body. Many of my clients have had awesome dates randomly fall into their laps during their Dating Detox. While detoxing, my client Christine was out with her friend and had a gorgeous man approach her and say, "You just look so joyful and beautiful. Can I take you out?"

If that happens and it feels right, go for it. But like Christine, you can also confidently say, "No, thanks, I'm good." Because you are in *your* right timing.

Use the time you would be swiping or dating to do things that bring you unequivocal *joy*. Do something silly, hilarious, playful, and fun—*just* for you. And understand that what is for you will still be there after this intentional break.

And bonus: the more well rested, well fed, and self-trusting you are as a woman, the more the patriarchy loses and you win.

THE ONE-MONTH DATING DETOX

For at least thirty days and while you read the next chapters, I invite you to take on the following three things:

Step One: Detox Your Dating Life

In Step One of this detox, I invite you to delete all your dating apps, stop going on dates,* put any flings or situationships you have on pause, and stop texting any exes or people you've been casually seeing.

---

* *In this time, if a date falls from the sky into your lap and the person feels aligned and exciting to you, go on the date and trust yourself.*

Deactivating your dating life will release you from distraction because flirty, nebulous, or nowhere conversations with people who aren't right (and never will be right) for you are noise pollution. They will get in the way of your clarity and disturb your clean air. Like VapoRub, taking the time to deactivate your dating life will allow you to breathe easy.

If you're worried about ghosting, you can send a simple message like this: "Hey, I need a dating breather, so I'm going to be MIA for the next month or so. Just wanted to let you know." Boom. Send. Then, if you want to take it a step further, with all the love in your heart, you can block their numbers. If you aren't good friends (healthy friendships only!) or coparenting with an ex, block their numbers and delete the thread. Get space. *You* are the *only* person who is in charge of who gets to contact you.

The right people for you are on the other side of you showing up for yourself.

Step Two: Detox Other People's Advice

It's time for you to become the expert of your dating life. Stop asking for dating feedback from people who aren't you.* Your friend's coworker's mom's path is not your path. You are on your own journey, and your timing is perfect for *you*. Set a boundary with anyone in your life who offers unsolicited dating advice.

If your mom, coworker, or friend wants to talk about your

---

* *The exception to this rule is me! Or a therapist or a coach whom you trust to give you guidance.*

dating life,* you can say, "I'm working on my dating life, and I've got this. Let's talk about something else."

Stop talking about dating with them altogether. This also means taking a break from talking about how "sucky" or "non-existent" dating is with friends, family, or coworkers who keep you in a negative loop that is not serving you or what you want in your dating life. If dating comes up in that circle over margaritas during your Dating Detox, you can say, "I'm doing some restorative rest in my dating life, so I'm trying not to speak negatively about it for a month."

Step Three: Detox from Dating Worry

This is the hardest step. First you have to get aware of the worries inside your brain about your dating life. Maybe you know them clearly. Maybe they're way beneath the surface and you've been pushing them away for years.

Time to bring them out into the light. Write out all your dating worries in a journal. What's the worst-case scenario? What are you worried is going to happen or not happen? The next time a worry thought pops up, say, "Hi!" to it. Don't try to just push it away. That only makes it bigger and scarier. Be a loving witness to your brain.

When you find yourself worrying, you can say the following:

> "I hear you thinking _____. That's a thought,
> not a fact. I get to choose again. I choose to believe
> that...

---

* Feel free to talk about your work inside this book with people you trust, but only if you want to.

THANK YOU, MORE PLEASE

"I am learning how to attract love.

"I am trustworthy.

"I have human thoughts and that's OK. I'm learning a new way to date.

"It might not be impossible that what is meant for me will not pass me by."

Use the language that feels most useful and true to you. Put it on your desktop screen or on a sticky note on your mirror. Remind yourself of this truth out loud and often.

MESSY HOMEWORK: The Dating Detox Journal

Every day for the next month, I want you to check in with yourself and how this Dating Detox is feeling. Even if it's just a sentence, write down what's coming up for you—whether that is excitement, fear, or both.

Don't worry about getting this (or any task I recommend in this book) done "perfectly." Perfectionism will just keep you stuck in inaction, which is why I've named this section in each chapter "Messy Homework." The goal is to take one messy, imperfect step forward with each chapter.

I know the concept of "being messy" has a dramatic, kinda negative connotation. Maybe a chaotic, getting-drunk-and-texting-your-ex kind of vibe. Underneath the surface is a woman who is bold, who has needs, and who is advocating for them. And while you might not want to drunk-text your ex (to be honest, you deserve better anyway), I want to give you a big permission slip to embody a new definition of "messy."

To me, "getting messy" means allowing and examining feelings you were socialized to hide or shrink because of your patriarchal conditioning. It means allowing yourself to be im-perfect, even though you were taught to survive with perfec-tionism. It means allowing yourself to take center stage in your own life, instead of defaulting to people-pleasing. So with that, let's get into the Messy Homework. This Dating Detox Journal will allow you to keep track of your detox progress so you have a log of your growth and a space to allow big feelings to come up. You can start by answering the following questions:

- How will this Dating Detox serve me?
- What permission do I need to give myself

to get the most out of this Dating
Detox?
- What's my support plan when (inevitably)
this Dating Detox gets tough? Examples
could include texting a friend and asking for
support, joyfully moving my body, taking deep
breaths, or doing my favorite form of self-
care.

Be bold, allow your big feelings, and dive in. Remember,
we're not going for "perfection" in this process. We're shoot-
ing for messy progress.

2

Release That Shit

YOUR DATING PATTERNS ARE HAUNTING YOU

Tell me if this sounds familiar: After years of trying (and not finding the right person), you go out on what you hope is a promising
date. You sit down, you think it goes well, and you go out again.
They didn't ask you that many questions, but they were really cute
and you thought there was potential. You keep seeing each other
and having some fun in the process. During the first date, they
told you that they wanted a relationship with "the right person."
You took that as a sign that *you* could be the "right person." You
tell all your friends (and yourself), "This one is different! They
want a relationship!"

You think "things are evolving in the right direction." But then six months into dating when they recoil at a party when you call them your "boyfriend/girlfriend," you realize that they didn't really want a relationship at all. You then put the clues together from your past dates and realize, "Oh shit, they have the emotional availability of a teaspoon. I've attracted someone emotionally unavailable and commitment-phobic *again*?!"

One minute you think, *I've done so much therapy. I'm over that pattern. I'm going to be with someone different next time.* And then, JUMP SCARE, seemingly from nowhere, another emotionally unavailable, immature, gaslighting, never-wanted-a-relationship, only-wants-a-hookup, your-needs-are-too-much person jumps out to prove that original fear right.

And you're on the run again. Fleeing from the ghosts and ghouls of your past, hoping to never run into one again.

All signs are pointing to these "truths": What you want is impossible. You'll be stuck in this cycle of attracting people that are wrong for you, forever. Dating is hopeless! Turn back now while you still can!

This was me. My dating-life patterns felt like I was being cursed to run forever in a never-ending haunted house.

I know I'm not alone. I polled my online community about what patterns they were being haunted by in their dating lives, and here were just some of the responses:

> *I crush only on people where there's an obstacle (e.g., I work with them).*

> *I'm attracted only to unavailable people.*

On dates, I care more about what they think of me than what I think of them.

I have a constant fear of being vulnerable and put too much pressure on myself.

I run when I feel it getting serious.

I overextend myself in dating because I'm begging them to love me.

I attract women who pursue me, but withdraw when I reciprocate feelings.

I attract the bare minimum, who think my needs are too much.

I feel so comfortable in single life (partly as a coping mechanism) that I avoid dating altogether.

I meet "good on paper" guys but I never feel a connection or sincere interest.

For me, I was haunted by my dating-life patterns for what seemed like an eternity. It felt like my curse in life was to attract people who believed I was "too much."

This pattern was perpetuated with every single romantic interaction I had—starting with Mason.

Mason and I got together when I was sixteen. He was hilarious, cute, and most importantly, super into me. This was a shock to my system. I felt like I'd won the lottery. SOMEONE LIKED ME! HE REALLY LIKED ME!

I immersed myself in his life, his friend group, his interests, and his family. It felt fucking fantastic to be chosen, especially by a boy. I thought being chosen by Mason would signal to everyone in my high school, "*Look!* She's not that weird because a boy has chosen to be with her" (*cough cough* insert patriarchal conditioning).

As this budding high school romance was building, my parents' relationship was crumbling. Mason was the first call I made after my parents sat me and my brother down and told us they were getting a divorce, the first time. (They would officially divorce again in my twenties and it was a horrible experience all over again.)

He was there to support me when, two weeks later, my best friend (and my only friend) told me she and her family were moving across the country. He was my rock when, horrifyingly, a roach fell on my naked shoulder the year we had to move into an infested home to avoid foreclosure. He became my lifeline. As Christian high schoolers in the Deep South who were dry humping constantly, there was only one thought on my mind: We *will* be married—and I was all in.

I did respond to Mason's abnormal-for-me love with some intensity. Like the time when I gave him a giant painting of us that was commissioned by one of my friends for our one-year anniversary. When I presented this gift to Mason, he promptly said, "Lily, why don't you keep that for your home?" (How dare he not take this *life-size* painting of us home to his tiny room?!)

And yes, I did write a one-hundred-page journal to him listing the reasons I loved him. (I got the idea after I saw someone do it for a proposal.) I gave this journal to Mason on the eve of his journey to college. He looked at the cover, didn't even crack the spine, and put it in the back of his closet. I felt like my heart was back there with that unread journal.

A few weeks later, a year and a half into this high school romance, Mason came over to my house and said, "You're just too much. I'm breaking up with you." To say I was crushed would be an understatement. This moment confirmed everything that I feared about myself. I took Mason's rejection to mean that I was too intense, too weird, too much, and loved too hard.

I desperately wanted to prove him wrong, so I went out into the dating world trying (and failing) to escape this "you're too much" pattern.

But I was thrown right back into my haunted house. The next kiss I had was in college with the only boy who expressed interest in me in four years of school. (This also felt like my curse. "Opportunities are *rare* when you are too much!")

We talked for hours, flirted hard-core, and then made out in his tiny dorm room. I was thinking, *Wahoo! A boy likes you! You have a connection! Maybe this could be something?* He told me the next day he had a girlfriend whom he'd cheated on with me. Fuck.

Years later there was Jack. I was living in San Francisco at the time in my first job as a college graduate. My friend Jessie invited me to a wine-tasting day at a vineyard in Napa (hello, fancy!), and I jumped at the opportunity. Jessie's roommate would drive.

Enter Jack. I was into him immediately. He was older, from the South, supersmart, and funny (just like me!?). It was fun and flirty right away. AND WHILE SIPPING WINE NO LESS. I was like, *Wait, am I quite literally living the dream?!*

When we got back to the city, our conversation progressed. He asked me on a date for that Sunday, and we started making out in his kitchen. *Hot.*

All signs were pointing to: *It's finally happening for you.*

I should have known something was off when Jack moved our brunch date up by three hours. To 8 a.m. I woke up at 6 a.m., took an hour to get ready, and showed up fifteen minutes early. He walked in ten minutes late, no smile or hug, got in line with me, and ordered a coffee for himself. I ordered one for me. He immediately made it clear that we were on separate checks (which I didn't mind), but I did find it weird that he felt the need to declare it loudly to the barista.

We sat outside, and he immediately said, "I can't be going on a date. I just got out of a long relationship. You're great and the other night was cool, but you're not for me."

WHAT THE ACTUAL FUCK?

How is it that I kept attracting men who rejected me almost immediately? Then when I had an actual relationship, they broke up with me saying I was "too much." This pattern felt like my fault. It felt like a *Groundhog Day* nightmare that I was bound to repeat forever.

I thought that to fix this pattern, I needed to "stop being too much." Stop asking for so much, be "more chill" (code for: "Don't ask for what you want, it's not cool"). Running away from the "too muchness" is what I thought would protect me from this pattern happening again.

I thought the tide was turning with Dylan, my relationship with whom you know from the last chapter ended in a fiery, messy hellscape. But at the beginning, things felt massively different. He liked my big personality. He liked that I was enthusiastic, a leader, and kind of bossy. I thought I'd finally outrun the "You attract people who believe you are too much" story.

But then it was back to the haunted house pattern.

Again and again. I abandoned myself and my needs in favor of this relationship. I had internalized the belief that I was too much and therefore deserved whatever scraps of love and belonging I got. I thought in order for the pattern to end, I had to lower my standards. I believed that being in a relationship proved that I was a worthy human being (a myth that the patriarchy has tried hard to push as truth), so I had to try *really* hard.

After things blew up and ended with Dylan, I knew something had to change. I was tired of running from the ghosts and ghouls inside the haunted house, taunting me for how alone and "too much" I was.

My nervous system was fried from all the sleepless nights and wondering if I was indeed "too much" for real partnership and romantic love. After years of being haunted by this pattern, I realized I couldn't outrun it. Shrinking and asking for less wasn't going to fix it.

To banish it for good, I had to turn on the light.

TURNING ON THE LIGHT

I could feel that my dating-life patterns were deeper than just a date. I wanted to find their source to figure out how to never attract that kind of situationship again.

I put on my best adventuring outfit and became Nicolas Cage in *National Treasure*, obsessed with decoding my patterns. I was willing to dive deep and find them at their source. The result became how I developed the Pattern Finder.

I went way back in my love-life past. Not just to the first date, but to the first time I was taught about romantic love. The first crush. The first time I was rejected. And here's what I found:

"I'm too much" was a pattern starting in first grade. I was at the lunch table, sitting with the girls, and a classmate of mine named Will was sitting with the boys. Will looked over and yelled, "Lily, will you go out with me?" Then all the boys started laughing hysterically. Then his friend gave him a five-dollar bill. They laughed at me and said, "It was a joke! I was paid to do that. You think I would want to go out with you?!" Enter the story that I am prank-worthy, but not "ask out"–worthy.

Then the belief pattern was cemented further at home. When I was twelve, my mom told me I would "have a hard time finding a husband because you're so much." This felt like being handed a life sentence of loneliness.

Next came my biggest-ever crush: Connor. At this point in my pattern hunt, the Hans Zimmer score builds, the tension could be cut with a knife, and we're getting close to the root of my pattern…

We were in sixth grade and the puberty hormones were flying. I remember looking up into the sky in my backyard and thinking on a crisp Wednesday afternoon, *What is Connor thinking about?* I would obsess over his gorgeous blond hair, his tall frame, and his drenched-in-coolness attitude. He was popular. I decidedly was not. While he was getting compliments on his Nike Shox (which were sold out everywhere), I was getting my books thrown in the boys' bathroom before class.

Then one day, my teacher moved around our sixth-grade class seating chart. And GUESS WHO I WAS SEATED RIGHT NEXT TO?! Connor.

I had my opportunity. He *was* going to fall in love with me and see how cool I could be. But the thing about me, I have always struggled putting my hand down and keeping quiet. So inevitably, my teacher's pet Hermione Granger not-coolness won out.

Another uncool thing that was happening in my life at the time was a ton of sweat and bacteria doing a new dance in my armpits. To add insult to injury, my mom insisted on buying Tom's of Maine natural deodorant, which, at this moment in time, only added a slight hint of patchouli to raging body odor. If anything, it enhanced my BO, which I was unaware of until one fateful Wednesday in class.

Gym was in the middle of the day in sixth grade (a true crime), and after we changed from playing some sort of game I was terrible at, I went back to my classroom to sit next to my megacrush. I was writing in my notebook when I looked over at Connor. The whole class was staring at us, which was confusing for a moment until I looked over at him. He was wordlessly waving his hand in front of his face with a disgusted look. It was a look that said, "She smells terrible."

A cold rush of embarrassment washed through my body. I went numb. I looked down, angled toward Connor, and said, "Connor, you think I smell bad?"

He, shocked that I caught him and so embarrassed he couldn't make eye contact said, "Yeah."

All I could say was, "Well, OK," and I turned around to sit in my BO shame as the whole class stared.

A few weeks later, I saw that the popular group of boys had brought Axe body spray to school (another crime). If you aren't aware (in which case you are truly lucky), Axe body spray is a product exclusively used by twelve-year-old boys in the early 2000s that has an offensive, violent odor whose scent profile can only be described as "douchy." I said what I said.

When her back was turned, they were spraying it on another girl in class who was deemed "smelly." They sprayed it all over her and her books when she wasn't looking. I felt so sad for her. And then an hour later, I realized that I smelled like Axe too. They had sprayed me all over with that nasty, overperfumed yuck.

After this incident, my thirteen-year-old self was emotionally demolished that my crush seemingly found me repulsive, *and* I was petrified of having BO. I saved up my allowance to buy the "clinical strength" deodorant from the store. Never mind the aluminum—*I must not stink.* I went to the bathroom at least two times per class, obsessively smelling my armpits to make sure they weren't offensive and that I wouldn't have to be ostracized in front of everyone again.

These traumatic moments developed into obsessive-compulsive tendencies. On field trips I begged a chaperone to check and make sure I wasn't emitting an odor. When I finally made a close friend the next year, in seventh grade, I insisted that she come to the bathroom with me every single class to check (and check again) that I didn't smell bad.

Yeah, it was a lot.

As an adult who has gone through years of therapy, I know now my brain organized these experiences to mean *everything* about my identity and what was possible for me. To keep me safe from future rejection a belief was formed—I was the stinky girl. The one who is and will always be "too much."

BOOM. There it was.

I realized that the pattern of attracting men who believed I was too much, who weren't ready for commitment, had *everything* to do with my dusty, crusty beliefs underneath the surface.

CHALLENGING OUR DUSTY, CRUSTY BELIEFS

I didn't just attract men who thought I was too much. I *believed* I was too much for true love and belonging.

Patterns are only as strong as the dusty, crusty beliefs backing them up (aka your brain's earnest and futile attempt at protecting you from rejection and future hurt forever). And trying to fix your dating-life patterns without working on the dusty, crusty beliefs underneath is like slapping new paint on the walls of a house with a crumbling foundation.

Instead of questioning the validity of the story itself, I centered it in my dating search efforts. This only attracted people for whom I was "too much." Cue foundation crumbling.

Brené Brown was right: "The most powerful stories may be the ones we tell ourselves. And they're usually fiction."

Here's how the most vicious, dusty, crusty beliefs are created in our dating lives:

Our brains are excellent storytellers and want to be right to keep us safe, beating the future crushes and dating prospects like Connor to the punch. Then they look for confirmation of that story to keep us in a predictable zone. If I believed that I was too much, then they couldn't hurt me as badly, right?

To continue to be safe, our brain engages in confirmation bias. In my case, I started to see and attract emotionally unavailable people and situationships *everywhere*, affirming the original pattern, triggering the dusty, crusty belief that "I *am* too much," and making it seem even more true.

Your family history might also be contributing to the dusty, crusty beliefs. There have been generations of women in our history who had to settle romantically to survive. Economic survival and social acceptance were, and in some cases still are, intimately interwoven with being legally partnered to a cisgender man.

This generational trauma was never clearer than when I asked my mom why she had told me at twelve that I was "too much and I was going to have a hard time finding a husband." She responded: "I was told that when I was twelve by a male family member." She then passed down that judgment to me. This was a tool she thought would be helpful to my survival in this patriarchal hellscape.

Hello, fuel on the fire.

Most people (including myself before doing this work), have attics so full of these dusty, crusty beliefs (the thoughts they've practiced a zillion times) about themselves and what is possible in their romantic life that they have become hoarders.

These beliefs might sound like the following:

> "What I want doesn't exist."

> "I'm too ambitious and people I'm attracted to are turned off by that."

> "I'm not thin enough, not pretty enough, or not laid-back enough for a relationship."

> "My friends found love so much easier than me, so there must be something wrong with me."

When these survival thoughts feel true, they usually throw their host into a panic-and-anxiety cocktail. This ushers our nervous systems into a full-out chorus line of fight, flight, freeze, or fawn mode to avoid rejection. Your brain fears rejection like it fears death. Back in the day for our cave-dwelling ancestors, rejection meant being put out of the cave and literally *dying* from exposure to the elements. So if we treat these thoughts as the truth, our nervous systems take them *very* seriously.

My intellectual, feminist brain would hear these dusty, crusty beliefs and fight back with her own aggressive opposite solo: "Fuck that. You don't need a man. You don't need to date. You are whole right now, so don't worry about it…"

The seesawing between these two ideas (called cognitive dissonance) was sucking the life out of me.

While my feminist brain was right—I was enough as I was, and I didn't need a romantic relationship to complete me—those aggressively opposite thoughts didn't fix the original dusty, crusty beliefs. It was stuck just going back and forth.

Our brains don't want to be wrong. It's like a well-intentioned helicopter parent, trying to protect her child at every cost but really just keeping the kid stuck in a plastic bubble.

Without getting all woo-woo here, your thoughts are incredibly powerful at creating your reality. When you think, *I'm just going to die alone,* your body has feelings pop up. These feelings might be associated with shame because you feel left behind or you feel self-blame. Maybe you choose to stay in bed most of the day. You might have mustered enough energy to push through, go on a bunch of dates, and try to prove that story wrong. But you end up in the same cycle of thoughts, feelings, and actions the next day. No matter how hard you hustle for something different, the pattern stays the same if you don't address the belief underneath.

These beliefs are like that moth-eaten ten-year-old sweater you have in the back of your closet. For years, it's just been gathering dust and taking up valuable closet real estate. But on that obsessive cleaning binge you have on a late Saturday in October, you come upon that sweater and find ten reasons to not throw it out. This old orange lump of wool holds a memory. You looked great in it once and it enveloped a younger you. But in reality, it's holding you back.

As you move forward in this book, you're going to want to

spring-clean that closet. We're about to gather so many more beautiful, powerful pieces that represent the *new*, fiercely confident, badass you.

Before we dive deeper, here's a caveat. There is a big difference between facts and the stories you tell yourself. The sky on planet Earth is blue. Water is wet. Racism, ableism, homophobia, transphobia, and fatphobia exist—and they make dating much harder for those they impact than for white, able-bodied, or straight or straight-presenting privilege. These are FACTS.

So, especially if you hold a marginalized identity, my intention is *not* to gaslight you into thinking that the only problem with your pattern is the story you're telling yourself. This shit is way more complex than that.

Instead, this is about learning what you *are* in control of. This process is about discovering what thoughts and stories *are* perpetuating your patterns and holding you back from learning to prioritize yourself in your experience of dating. You will learn how to center *your* needs, how to never settle, and how to trust your body to lead you in the right direction for you.

So how the hell can you unbelieve these dusty, crusty, unhelpful, passed-down, overly protective, fearful helicopter-parent thoughts about yourself?

RELEASING THAT SHIT

Healing your patterns means releasing and rewriting the dusty, crusty beliefs that no longer serve you. It means creating safety in your body to process everything that feels sticky from your love-life past and healing the legacy of settling that has been handed down to you.

What you believe about yourself and your love life means everything to breaking your patterns.

Let me give you an example. Danielle is a badass working in education. When we met, she had just broken up with a toxic, emotionally abusive partner.

Her therapist recommended she speak with me, and we set up a call. The first time we spoke, she sat in her car after a hard day of work, with cold rain pouring outside. Corny as it sounds, the weather was an appropriate reflection of the hard-as-shit feelings she was going through.

She was petrified of repeating her pattern of falling for someone who could be so wrong for her. After being gaslit for so long by a romantic partner, she felt unsafe trusting her love-life decision-making. She felt shame for being with the wrong partner for so long. She was afraid to trust herself.

Then, in response, her high-achieving feminist brain would kick up its defenses and say to me: "These are silly worries! I shouldn't worry about this. I should have this figured out by now. I know I've got this!" Her brain would oscillate like a seesaw between these two extremes.

The dusty, crusty survival story underneath the surface for Danielle was this: "I cannot be trusted. What I want isn't possible."

And it was time to heal and rewrite that shit.

This is where the magic happens.

The first step to healing that shit is *not* to use toxic positivity as your way out of the old patterns and survival stories. Toxic positivity sounds like, "Next time will be better! EVERYTHING IS FINE!" (Insert forced smile.)

> **Toxic positivity is like an off-brand cheap plastic Band-Aid. It will fall off the minute you're in hot water.**

The answer is also not to shove the survival stories in a closet and hope they will go away when you find a relationship. (Heads up: Your survival stories and old harmful coping mechanisms *will* follow you into that relationship. So you better rewrite that shit now.)

We're here to create a deeper solution. Here are the two tools I taught Danielle so she could stop her pattern in its tracks *and* rewrite her beliefs.

1. Practicing self-compassion
2. Creating baby-step reframes

Practicing Self-Compassion

So many of us ambitious, high-achieving women were taught to survive by being excellent at everything. The need for this behavior is even further exacerbated for those who hold marginalized identities. And if dating feels like the one place that you don't know what you're doing, you might have responded with some hard-core self-blame.

A Stanford University study in 2014 showed that "self-criticism makes us weaker in the face of failure, more emotional, and less likely to assimilate lessons from our failures." Self-blame often shows up and slows you down when you are faced with your old patterns.

The capitalist patriarchy has socialized us all to value hustle, perfectionism, achievement, and pushing through as the answer. We're taught to believe that exercising softness, tenderness, and slowness with ourselves is weak. That's bullshit.

Dr. Kristin Neff, a self-compassion expert, TED talk star, and author, explains, "Instead of mercilessly judging and criticizing yourself...self-compassion means you are kind and understanding when confronted with personal failings—after all, who ever said you were supposed to be perfect?"

This same Stanford study found that the practice of self-compassion leads to increased resiliency (in other words, getting you out there to find the *best* relationship of your life) and decreased stress (aka more fucking joy in the process).

Self-compassion is like your best friend who knows how to lovingly sit next to you on a park bench and always knows the most comforting things to say.

Self-compassion in action looks like the following three things:

1. **The Kindest, Most Real "Of Course"** Give yourself the benefit of your context. "Of course I'm struggling with this dusty, crusty belief. I feel shame coming up like hot lava, and that sucks. Of course I've struggled with this pattern. I was taught that wanting what I wanted is selfish."

2. **Admitting Hard Thoughts** Mindfulness doesn't have to be a ten-minute meditation. Mindfulness can literally be you noticing that a dusty, crusty belief is coming up in your brain. You can simply say, "Whoop, I just had the thought that 'I should be in a relationship by now and my singleness is totally my fault.'" That's a thought, not a fact, and you can remind yourself of that. You don't have to identify with that thought as "truth." It's a passing survival mechanism, which you're learning to be safe without. This is being a loving witness to your human brain, instead of being a judgy, hangry critic.

3. **Recognizing That You're Not Alone** There are literally millions of people on this Earth who join you in hard-as-hell human thoughts and hard-as-fuck feelings. This is not to minimize your experience; it's about bringing you into the collective. You are not alone.

To practice self-compassion, you can use the prompts in this section to write yourself a self-compassion letter or recite aloud one of your favorite self-compassion mantras. When I'm being hard on myself, one of my favorite mantras to say out loud is "I am here for you and love you no matter what you feel, think, or do."

Self-compassion gives you the emotional safety you need to perform the second important step to rewriting that shit.

Creating Baby-Step Reframes

After dissolving your anxiety and stress with that self-compassion practice, you're ready to start building a new neural pathway (or thought pattern). One that actually supports what you want and actively builds hope. These new thoughts and beliefs will give you the juice you need to take courageous action and attract an amazing relationship.

Why hasn't building positive thoughts worked for you in the past? Because you've been trying to just jump to a positive thought without building the baby steps to get there. That's like getting a gym membership and trying to deadlift two hundred pounds on the first day. It's not going to work. Your body will be like, "WTF is happening?" Same with your brain. You need baby steps forward and practice to create new beliefs.

Building a new path, particularly one that supports your innate worthiness and actually helps create a new pattern of attracting amazing people, takes consistent work. You just have to go one step at a time.

I like to say that this work is an unhurried unfolding. It's OK to be in progress.

For Danielle, taking baby steps looked like moving from her well-worn neural pathway—"I'm the problem in my dating life! I'm behind everyone else in my life who is coupled!"—built after years of being in the wrong relationships, to practicing self-compassion. Then she could ask herself, "What else might be true?" To build a new belief and a new neural pathway, she needed to take baby steps. The aggressively positive thoughts like *Everything is going to be OK! You'll definitely meet someone else!* did not feel true to

Danielle. So we didn't pressure her brain to get there. Instead, we brainstormed some baby-step thoughts. Here's what we came up with:

> "It might not be impossible that I am learning the skill of trusting myself."
>
> "I am creating safety for myself."
>
> "It might be possible that my timing is right for me."
>
> "It's possible that I haven't met the right person yet."

The goal is to start with these baby step thoughts and then when they feel true, you're on your way up to the desired belief (aka, *It's inevitable that I find the right partner.*)

Danielle chose these baby-step thoughts and started practicing them hard-core. She wrote them down on sticky notes and put them all around her house. She made these thoughts a scrolling sentence on her phone's home screen. She repeated them out loud and often.

When her brain inevitably served up the old, *You're behind! It's your fault you're single! You're not to be trusted!* she practiced self-compassion and responded with, *I'm having a hard thought right now.* Then she practiced the baby-step reframing again.

The really cool product of this work is that your brain will eventually get used to a softer, safer climb up to a new belief about yourself and what's possible. Because after Danielle practiced "It might be possible that my timing is right," out loud and often, that thought eventually felt like, *Duh, that's obviously true.* This was her sign to start practicing a step up from that to: *My timing is right for me.*

After doing this for about a month, Danielle felt safe trying new, courageous stuff in her dating life. She claimed her Essence-Based Preferences (which we will discuss more in chapter 4) with massive permission. Danielle started asking for exactly what she wanted. She felt safe with these tools to start dating, and she was no longer paralyzed by the fear of settling for less again. She knew she completely had her own back.

And then Danielle met the love of her life, Bryan. Bryan was someone who showed her so much consistent, compassionate affection and love. This was something Danielle and her nervous system could now completely accept and receive.

For me, taking baby steps in my reframing process meant completely rewriting the "I'm too much" story and thereby banishing the pattern of attracting emotionally unavailable men.

The first baby-step thought I came up with was: *It might be true that if someone thinks that I'm too much, they are disqualified from my dating life.*

This one baby-step thought, practiced out loud and often, whenever I was lonely, triggered, or in the bathroom on a bad date, started creating a new neural pathway.

Then I upleveled to working on: *If they think I'm too much, then they are not enough for me.*

BOOM.

Enter a new neural pathway. I was now able to create a new pattern of setting more boundaries with people who weren't right for me. It felt good to ask for what I wanted out loud and often. Success looked like feeling free, boundaried as hell, and joyful in every aspect of my dating life. And the bonus was meeting my husband, Chris.

Now it's your turn. Let's do this.

MESSY HOMEWORK: Releasing Your Patterns Journal

For the next seven days, I challenge you to go on a pattern-finding mission. You can do this exercise in your journal and note your progress. Ask yourself these questions:

1. What patterns do I want to rewrite in my dating life?
2. What experience (or experiences) is (are) at the root of this pattern?
3. What dusty, crusty beliefs about me are under the surface?
4. What might self-compassion say?
5. What else might be true? What's a baby-step reframe I can practice here?

Remember, take action, and do it imperfectly. Give yourself all the permission, allow all the big feelings, and show up for yourself. That lovingly messy energy is what creates results, so let's go.

3

The Brazen Bragging Revolution

You may have been taught that bragging was bad. It meant you were cocky and full of yourself. It meant that you were no different from those sleazy finance bros sucking all the air out of the room with talk of the returns on their stock portfolio last year. Nobody cares, Dan!

"Bro bragging" is air-sucking nonsense, designed to make the bragger feel big and others feel small. It's a symptom of the hierarchical, capitalistic patriarchy, in which we know our worth by how much is in our bank accounts. It's bullshit—and it's absolutely not what I'm talking about.

What I'm talking about is Brazen Bragging, which combats a very real problem. We as women were not taught how to center ourselves, our needs, our desires, and our pleasure, especially in our love lives. This is because of the myriad oppressive forces socializing you to play small, ask for less, shrink your needs, and be "less intimidating" to be more appealing. And it's also bullshit.

It's like that moment in my favorite rom-com, *The Holiday*. The glowing, cashmere-drenched Cameron Diaz has just hooked up with the stunning, stubble-sporting Jude Law in the sexiest one-night stand, and then they start dating, even though she's only in England for one more week (GASP). On one of these dates, Cameron basically says, "I know I told you I *work* for a company, but I'm really the founder and CEO. I didn't share because that intimidates some guys."

Cameron's character had learned, probably through a lot of shitty dating situations, to hide her achievements, her job, and her brags because doing so was the price of romantic connection with men. This kind of learned safety mechanism is not serving her, nor is it serving you.

Hiding your full awesomeness is a one-way ticket to unfulfilling dates and uninspiring relationships. I don't want you to hide your accomplishments, your badassery, your growth, your progress, or your ambition for anyone any longer. Bragging is the key not only to a joyful dating life, but also to attracting the person who is uniquely qualified for you.

Brazen Bragging is super uncomfortable for most, and life-changing for all who try it. Why? When you shift the focus of your dating life from "Do they like me?" to "Here's exactly why I love myself and here's exactly why I'm awesome," dating becomes an act of self-love and self-care.

Brazen Bragging is revolutionary. It's learning to take up your space. It's knowing what you bring to the table and being able to proudly talk about it. This kind of bragging magnetizes the right people to you and repels the rest.

Before we get to "how," let's talk about why you might have wanted to throw this book across the room when I said you should start bragging:

Growing up in the South, I dared not brag about myself. I heard messages such as "Don't brag, it's unladylike. It's arrogant," or "Talking about your accomplishments is intimidating and pushes people away." Talking about my accomplishments felt like a secret only for inside my home. My parents were super celebratory of me and my brother as kids. They made me a participation medal for my first-grade ballet recital (I'm a classic millennial).

But around me at school, at my friends' homes, and at church, it was a different story. I never saw women celebrating their accomplishments. In these spaces "feminism" was also a dirty word (definitely not a coincidence). The only acknowledgment I saw women receive was at their wedding. The only moment a woman could brag about was when she decided to chain herself...I mean "get engaged" to a cisgender, heterosexual man.

In the words of Bianca Del Rio, Not today, Satan.

My hesitance to brag completely broke during my sophomore year of college. I went to school in Mississippi and chose to be in a sorority. (This was a very out-of-character move for me, but I was desperate for friendship in a sea of strangers.) I got chosen by one, joined, and fell in line with its rules and structures. There were some good times. Like laughing with the seniors who took me under their wing and making out with some fellow members at our formals. (Did I mention I didn't yet know I was bisexual? The writing was on the wall with that one.)

There was a supersecret hundred-year-old ceremony (no, we did not drink any blood or perform a ritual sacrifice), which was called Candlelight. (Will the sorority standards counsel get mad at me for writing this in my book? Come at me!) Here's how it went down.

You would be called to the sorority house for an urgent meeting. The lights would go off. The room would fall into a knowing, excited hush. Everyone would stand in a circle, and the president would light a candle. The number of times the candle went around the circle without being blown out would signify what we were celebrating. You ready for a blast from the past?

One circle around meant a man in a fraternity had "pinned" you. He would give you his frat pin as a promise-ring type thing. God bless.

Two times around the circle signified that someone had gotten engaged. Then that person would blow out the candle, the room would erupt into piercing screams of joy, and her sisters would run to her feet and ask "HOW DID IT HAPPEN?" She would then gleefully take out her engagement ring and tell the whole story.

The first time this happened was my freshman year, and I was right in the middle of the pack, cheering and begging for the story alongside my sisters. The third time it happened I was more tentative, watching it unfold from the back of the seated pack.

The fifth time, I didn't sit. I put on my most appropriately supportive face and stood at the back, taking the role of anthropologist. It was an odd experience. I watched the screaming with joy, the rushing to her feet, the "Tell us the story!," and found myself growing angry. Not because the engagement happened, not because I was jealous of these relationships (to be honest, I did not find many of the men at my college appealing). I was noticing that *this* moment was the most excited our group ever was. It was the most celebration a woman in our sorority ever received. That struck me as odd, wrong even.

It also was gross to me that the moment we most celebrated in this body of badass women was the moment they got engaged. Sure, there were snaps for other kinds of celebrations, but not in this same full-bodied, gleeful, giant way.

Here's my (very much not an expert) anthropological breakdown of the piercing screams of joy in response to Candlelight:

1. Romantic love is fun. Celebrating romantic love can be fun.
2. As a room full of just-out-of-high-school babies, it was fun being more adult. And what is more adult than deciding to marry someone?
3. And the big one: As a woman in the South especially, getting married to a cisgender, straight man makes you more valuable to society, and in some cases more valuable to your family. Whether consciously or unconsciously, this group of women, me included, knew that.

This intense focus on the heteronormative performance of romantic love as a marker for your worth as a woman is also why it took me years to realize I was officially not straight and to come out as bisexual. Growing up, I had crushes on other girls, but I felt paralyzed from acting on them. Looking around, there weren't many (if any) examples of women who were fluid in their sexuality. I also was raised in Alabama in the 1990s and early 2000s, where if anyone at my school caught a whiff of another student having interest in the same sex, ostracization would occur. I saw it happen again and again. And after so much rejection from my male crushes, I doubted my own attraction to other people, especially women. It took me decades to realize that most women around me were also queer.

The heteronormative socialization and internalized homophobia I experienced were real. It took a really intense crush on a woman in my acting class when I first moved to New York to allow my brain to catch up to what my heart had known for a long time. I came out as bisexual to my parents and friends shortly before I met Chris, my now husband.

Now, back to the Mississippi sorority...

There were so many women in the room I looked up to. Beyond getting engaged, they were doing badass things in their careers, their majors, and our community. They were landing amazing internships and jobs and getting clarity on what they wanted to do with their lives. I wanted to cheer and run to their feet and ask them to tell me the story of how they landed that internship at the Met. I was also aware that one hundred years prior, when this Candlelight tradition was born, a woman didn't have many options outside of marriage. I was hungry for a symbolic and tangible shift in how we celebrated ourselves and one another, one that reflected my view of what twenty-first-century womanhood meant.

So, after the fifth Candlelight in four months, I decided to take my frustration and spearhead a solution. I started an informal campaign to start a new tradition. To supplement Candlelight with other types of celebration for career and life wins. I started with my closest friends in the sorority, telling them my idea. They seemed tentatively supportive, so I took that as a sign to keep going. I became Norma Rae in the cafeteria, sharing this idea with older members of the sorority, and gaining traction and support. Or so I thought.

My pitch was something like, "There are so many women doing incredible things inside this group. Why don't we start a new tradition to celebrate them like we do at Candlelight? I know that women especially in the South have trouble celebrating themselves, so I can go first, then I know five other women who are doing amazing things and want to celebrate."

Looking back, I realize that offering to celebrate myself at all was a big mistake in my bid to get a new tradition started in this hundred-year-old organization in Mississippi. For context, my life had just changed drastically; I had landed a huge opportunity to go and blog for an international women's rights conference in Istanbul, Turkey. And goddamn it, I wanted to celebrate. This would later be used against me by the powers that be inside the sorority. How dare a woman want to celebrate herself? Everything must be for others!

I was in my car, on the way to the airport to go to Istanbul, when I got a call from the president of my sorority.

"Can you talk?" she said in a syrupy, sweet voice.

"Sure, what's up?" I responded naively.

"Some people from the chapter have been telling me that you want to start a new Candlelight tradition to celebrate career wins. Lily, that will never happen. This is a one-hundred-year-old organization, and this tradition will never change. Did you know that marriage is a sacrament in my religion? Obviously career wins are nowhere near as important as choosing to marry someone. Also, did you ever think about how your idea would hurt the women who are engaged and who had a Candlelight ceremony? By the way, you know some people thought you were self-aggrandizing by wanting to celebrate yourself. You should really stop talking about this new idea because it's never going to happen."

I was in complete shock. I wish I could tell you that I said, "OK, well, fuck you and that sorority. I quit." But I didn't. Instead, my people-pleasing survival skills kicked in. The friends I thought I'd made inside the sorority, whom I'd shared my idea with, flashed before my eyes. I cried and apologized for hurting anyone's feelings. I felt utterly alone and filled with shame.

FALLING INTO THE PEOPLE-PLEASING TRAP

On the plane to Istanbul, I punished myself for being so bold, thinking about every person and every "friend" who might have been talking behind my back about what a "self-aggrandizing" (read: bad) woman I was.

This people-pleasing trap had kept me stuck for decades. It

was a survival skill I was good at putting on. It was like a really starchy, stiff Easter dress that would impress the old women at my church. I had seen every single woman in my family play the people-pleasing game so well. And when one stepped a toe out of that people-pleasing line, she got a slap on the wrist from older male (and sometimes female) members of the family. This legacy of being "accommodating" and "pleasing" had seeped into every pore of my skin. But I could feel a big change brewing.

After the shock of that conversation wore off, on the plane on my way to this conference, I asked myself: Why had I bowed to the whims of this sorority president who I didn't respect or even like? The answer came quickly: Because I deeply desired belonging. Even though that group was not in alignment with my personal values, I was willing to trade my comfort for a seat at the lunch table.

When I arrived in Istanbul, I immediately met Egyptian women who were protesting for their basic human rights, survivors of sexual assault, and children who took to stages and demanded change for their home countries. I interviewed as many women as I could and put their stories into my imperfect and earnest blog posts. I got to witness intersectional feminism in action, and it was life-changing.

One evening, I was journaling about these two wildly different realities I was living. I felt like a southern version of Hannah Montana. The brunette, "everyday" wig was for this weird universe in Mississippi where I'd just been slapped on the wrist for trying to start a new tradition to celebrate women outside of

THANK YOU, MORE PLEASE

marriage. The blond superstar wig was me watching the most powerful women I'd met in my whole life demand action and change from male-dominated, oppressive forces, literally risking their lives to do so.

I saw how much bigger the world was than the people who wanted women to play small. I was seeing in real time how taking up space as a woman was life-changing and, in so many cases, lifesaving.

I'm not saying that bragging about yourself is equivalent to fighting for human rights. What I am saying is that the way we do one thing is the way we do everything. I was learning that our ability to own what makes us awesome and courageous and then encouraging other women to do the same is a reciprocal force that generates the deepest belonging, the most joyful relationships, and the most profound change—with ourselves and others.

I quit the sorority two months after this incident. What I learned in just two years inside is how much our society abhors publicly celebrating women (or, God forbid, witnessing women's self-celebration) succeeding outside of established norms (i.e., the "Ladder of Life Achievement": engagement, marriage, babies, rinse, repeat).

We need a bragging revolution.

HOW TO BRAZENLY BRAG

This Mississippi sorority moment was the birthplace of my Brazen Bragging manifesto.

It's time for you to create your own massive celebration. Your ability to know and claim how amazing you are will have a direct impact on how you live your best freaking life possible and how you attract the best relationship of your life.

Knowing exactly what you bring to the table in relationships—with yourself and others—is what makes you uniquely qualified and more likely to attract the best friendships, jobs, and romantic relationships.

Giving yourself permission to brag about yourself will change everything about your love life. It will also mean quitting any sororities, relationships, and soul-sucking structures that don't champion the people inside them. It also will call you to invite the people you love to brag about themselves. Brazen Bragging doesn't suck the air out of the room—it adds breath and life to the right conversations and connections.

I'm speaking from my own experience. When I learned how to brazenly brag, it became a celebratory, tactical force in my dating life that attracted the right people and repelled the rest. This practice was directly responsible for attracting the life I wanted. I was aware of my brags. I celebrated them often. I invited everyone around me to do the same for themselves.

Getting to this place means doing something that will feel like nails on a chalkboard to any woman socialized like I was to put others' needs above her own: You're going to have to center yourself. You are uniquely qualified for the love of your life. Finding that person, or those people, for you, will become more easeful and speedier when you finally get selfish.

Your love life deserves your selfishness. You are deserving of

THANK YOU, MORE PLEASE

the love life you desire. This is our one wild life. Why would you settle for someone who selfishly is not your best-case scenario? Maybe because you aren't sure your best-case-scenario person even exists. I've seen too many people land in "Oh my god, I can't believe this exists!" relationships to let you live under that lie for a second longer.

> **"Selfish" is only a dirty word for people and systems invested in seeing you shrink.**

You picked up this bold-ass book because you're done shrinking, especially in your love life, right? So it's time to start bragging.

I'm not talking about building up a holier-than-thou personality, turning your nose up at everyone who is not you (that's the old, antiquated definition of bragging). Again, Brazen Bragging is breath. It's about knowing what you bring to the table and being really curious about the magic of those around you.

Brazen Bragging might feel uncomfortable or even sometimes unsafe. Those are normal feelings in response to a culture that is obviously hostile toward women and folks with marginalized identities occupying their power (or even their literal bodies).

That is why you don't go on this journey alone. This book reflects a feminist movement of women asking for more and boldly taking up space. This is why every single meeting or coaching session at my company, Date Brazen, starts with a bragging session. Every single person is asked to brag about something that they've done or that they want to celebrate. Afterward, the chat lights up with affirmation and celebration of that human. Everyone's brag, whether it's "I did a dance break at work and felt better," or "I just bought a house," or "I set a boundary with my mom," is celebrated equally. There is no brag too big or too small. Own every celebration, every win, and everything that makes you *you*. They are all steps to centering yourself and attracting someone for whom *you* are their best-case scenario.

WHAT IF BRAGGING FEELS WEIRD?

I recently had an aha moment in a Zoom accountability group. This group is how I stayed accountable to writing the stunning book you now hold in your hands. Before diving into deep work, we were asked to share in a small group, "What are you working on?" My instinct was to say something like, "I'm doing some writing" with a "no big deal, it's nothing" tone of voice. I had been to many virtual accountability groups while working on this book and had shared this nonchalant update dozens of times.

Then I realized, I'm couching in modesty what I am *actually* doing for fear of what these strangers will think of me. The thought I noticed in my brain sounded like, *Who are you to say you're writing a book? People will think you're full of yourself and self-aggrandizing!*

And I was literally writing a chapter on how to shed people-pleasing and brazenly brag! Let me tell you, dear reader, old trauma and socialization take a long time to unwind. The goal is *not* to never feel weird or nervous about bragging. The goal is to notice these human thoughts, practice compassion for them, and advocate for yourself anyway.

This time instead of my nonchalant "no big deal" share, I took a deep breath and said, "I'm working on a chapter of my book." I felt so proud. I also realized that it absolutely doesn't matter what these two strangers think of me.

You might get into a stickier situation than two strangers in a two-minute Zoom breakout room. Maybe you want to share a brag to a friend and you fear they'll be discouraging. Or you share a big win in a room full of family and they scoff. These two things have happened to me, and they suck. It's why I created a place where people are encouraged to brag every day. This practice takes time to normalize. Learning how to brazenly brag is not for the faint of heart. It's going to make some people uncomfortable. Hell, it will probably make *you* uncomfortable.

Some friends and family might not be ready to brag about themselves, and they might not be ready to receive your brag or celebration. We've all been programmed in this *Matrix*-ass reality to take up less space, celebrate marriage and babies above all else, and stop bragging because it's "unladylike." So there will be weird moments as you navigate unlearning this bullshit for yourself and invite others around you to do the same. Choose your community with care and only share with folks you feel safe with. You deserve support and belonging with the right people as you celebrate yourself growing bigger and bigger.

Taking up more space is going to be an imperfect, weird process for us all. Embrace the weird. Embrace the uncomfortable. Have compassion for that version of you who is still scared to brag about herself. The more you practice and figure out *your* version of Brazen Bragging, the more you will find people who celebrate alongside you.

Brazen Bragging isn't only about accomplishments or external things that are measurable—it's not just about your job, your bank account, or your upcoming vacation. Brazen Bragging is also about the intangible. It's about treating yourself with kindness, practicing self-compassion in a hard moment, setting a boundary to protect your peace, and vulnerably showing up to your latest therapy session. Learning this skill will change how you attract and go on dates. It will also create an environment that is supportive of you and everyone around you thriving. Here's how to identify your brags and how to use them as your dating superpower.

Use a Yes/And Approach

I love improv comedy so freaking much. I took a class for a year when I lived in San Francisco and learning that structure of play changed my life. One of the biggest "rules" of improv is "yes/and." When you're onstage doing a scene and your scene partner says, "Oh my goodness, what a gorgeous dress you're wearing!" You will "yes/and" the shit out of them by saying, "*Yes*, I love these sequins so much—*and* they make me feel like a fairy." The way to be a bad improv partner is to say, "No, I'm not wearing a dress, I'm wearing a tuxedo!" That's not playing; that's not fun.

Same for your dating life and bragging. The point is not to suck all the air out of the room by talking about yourself forever. It's to use bragging to "yes/and" conversations. Here are a few ways to practice using bragging to build deeper connection:

At your next friend hangout, ask, "What are you really proud of lately?" or "Do you have any brags that you want to share? I'd love to start a brag celebration with each other."

Or be *really* vulnerable and lead with: "I'm practicing the skill of bragging about myself. Would you mind if I shared a celebration with you?" *And* then follow up by asking what your friend would like to brag about.

On a date this sounds like asking something like, "What are you really proud of lately?"

Allow your date to answer, get really curious about their response, and then allow them to ask you the same question. Take up your freaking space and share your own brag!

That's "yes/and"-ing in practice; it's getting out of judgment and into curiosity. It's about how you communicate generously and joyfully in your love life, with yourself and potential partners. I will also share more in chapter 4 about the "both/and" approach, which is more internal. The "both/and" is about how you hold expansive space in your brain for all the thoughts and feelings you have with compassion (even when they feel messy or oppositional).

When you approach bragging with judgment, it sounds like, "I don't think they like me," or "I'm fucking this date up. I'm so weird..." What if you were to show up to a date knowing you are worthy of exactly what you desire, being grounded in what you want, and being genuinely curious about the other person? What if you took the pressure off them to prove to you that what you want exists? What if a date was just a game of "yes/and"?

Play to the Top of Your Intelligence

This is another improv rule that I *love*. Don't be afraid to intimidate. Don't couch your celebration or accomplishment in modesty for the comfort of others. Here's why.

I had a client, Rebecca, who owned her home in a really nice neighborhood in a big city, something she was very proud to have created for herself. On at least two dates with different people, when she shared that she was a homeowner, they would bristle, get defensive and comparative, and start talking about their accomplishments with an air of "I'm just as good as you."

Rebecca came to our session and shared that these moments made her feel like crap. They turned what was a fun, frothy date into a pissing contest that she didn't even want. "Maybe I shouldn't mention that I'm a homeowner until the third date? Maybe it's too intimidating."

My answer: "If your brag is intimidating to someone, why would they be the right person for you?"

She replied, "But I'm not looking for someone who makes as much money as me. I'm not looking for someone who also is a homeowner. I don't want to limit my pool that much."

I said, "You are looking for someone who is secure in themselves. Who can celebrate your wins with you. And who can clearly articulate their own wins. Who isn't competing with you for anything. Sharing what you were proud of allowed him to disqualify himself from your dating pool. For the right person, your celebrations will be just that—celebrations. Just as their celebrations will be celebrated by you."

Bragging can be the ultimate disqualifier of the wrong people for you. And the ultimate qualifier of the right ones too.

Playing to the top of your intelligence says you deserve to get what you want. If someone thinks you're too much, they are not enough for you.

When the pain of staying small, of trying not to intimidate, is greater than the fear of rejection, that's when you know it's time to start stepping onto a bigger stage.

In the next chapters, we'll integrate your brags into every moment of your dating strategy. From your in-person dating life to online, bragging is going to help you magnetize the right people to you and repel the rest.

But more importantly, bragging will help you reorganize your love life around yourself, your unique sparkle, and what you are bringing to the table. You are amazing, and this bragging skill will help you bring that amazingness into your love life with ease.

MESSY HOMEWORK: The Twenty in Two Challenge

For the next week, do this exercise every day. Set a two-minute timer and write twenty things you love about yourself. No pressure if you don't get to twenty—remember, don't get stuck in perfectionism. Do it messy!

Bragging doesn't just have to be about your achievements. This practice is not about the size of the brag; it's about cultivating the art of self-celebration. There are *so* many things you could brag about, and if you're stuck, here are some Brag-agories (like "categories," get it?):

Brag about your wins. This could include how you're growing, where you're thriving, celebrating a courageous moment you moved through, or anywhere that you're just really proud of yourself.

Brag about your essence. This could include your personality traits, your deeply rooted values, or what makes you a good friend. If I created an Essence-Based Preferences list (which we will learn about more in chapter 4) that was all about *you*, what would it include?

Brag about what you like about yourself. This could include your gorgeous eyes, your luscious hips, your voracious reading habit, your compassion, your ability to name the exact episode and season of *Gilmore Girls* by hearing just one line, or your you-ness.

There is literally no limit to what you can brag about.

Afterward, ask yourself these questions:

- What thoughts came up about yourself and about your brags?

- What feelings arose when you were making your list?
- How do you think recognizing and celebrating your brags would impact your dating life (and life in general)?

You can use this Twenty in Two Challenge to supercharge your dating life by doing it before swiping or before a date to get really clear on how awesome you are.

I dare you to brag on yourself with twenty in two in the space below right now. Ready, set, go!

4

Want More Than the Bare Minimum (aka Someone with a Job Who Is Nice)

Finding love means you gotta get more picky.

Gasp!

I know you've probably heard and internalized the advice that says, "Don't be too picky!" The assumption here is that wanting what you want will limit your options so much that you will completely fuck over the right person for you. You'll pass them over and will be left a shriveled, lonely old spinster because you dared to have clear preferences. How *dare* you want what you want?

This is bullshit.

"You're too picky" was born in the fiery hellscape of the patriarchy. "Picky" is just the word "pick" with a "y" at the end. It's like the word "needy," which literally vilifies you for *daring* to have needs, or like the word "moody," which judges you for being a human with a personality. You are *choosing* for yourself and expressing your agency by asking for what you want. This means you will probably challenge existing orders of power along the way and will no longer be waiting around for the permission of others to ask for and have what you want.

Choosing who you want is your literal right.

You might have been told or taught that your preferences were the "problem." You might believe that all relationships require work, so you might as well settle down with someone just good enough.

Did you watch the Oscars in 2013? If not, let me catch you up. Jennifer Garner was there with her then husband, Ben Affleck.

Ben won an Oscar for his film *Argo*, and at the end of his acceptance speech he turned to Jennifer, and in a very sweaty, excited, and panicked voice he said, "I want to thank my wife for working on our marriage for ten Christmases. It's work but it's the best kind of work, and there's no one I'd rather work with!"

They divorced a few years later.

As an adult child of divorce, I know that divorce can be a great thing. It can be a powerful force of agency, especially for women, who, until pretty recently, were severely limited in their ability to make that decision for themselves.

But this moment on live, internationally broadcast television sent a knowing chill down my spine. Maybe I'm just projecting, but to me the vibe was "The only thing I can say about my relationship is that it is hard."

What I saw from Jen G and Ben Affleck, my parents' arduous marriage, and women dying on the vine in long-term romantic relationships all around me was that all relationships are this hard.

I thought, *I might as well just settle down with someone who is just OK and do hard work for the rest of my life.* This kind of thinking led directly to me settling for that toxic relationship with Dylan a few years later.

This "settle for good enough" message was reinforced by friends and family who said things like, "Oh well, everyone's human; maybe you just need to give them another chance!" The answer to attracting the right partner isn't a vague, underfunctioning, open-minded list. It also isn't a rigid, overfunctioning snapshot of the exact height, graduating GPA, or hair length of your future partner.

The answer to attracting the right person is defining your Essence-Based Preferences (or EBPs).

EBPs are the living, breathing documentation of your desires that epitomize what would make you come alive across the table on a date and in the right relationship. This is your love-life vocabulary, and when you define it, this level of clarity will help you find the right person with more ease.

Without EBPs, most daters are swimming in indecision and self-doubt and giving the wrong people too many chances.

EBPs create a clear vision of how it feels to be with the right person for you, like a beautiful impressionist painting. There's this gorgeous impressionist painting by Renoir called *Luncheon of the Boating Party*. The painting features a bunch of women and men eating, a woman about to kiss her dog on the mouth (yuck), and a bunch of flirting and laughing. This isn't a Polaroid picture; it's not a rigid snapshot. But this impressionist painting gives you the feeling of being there.

With your EBPs, you'll capture the feeling of being in the right relationship, on the right date. You'll know how your future partner shows up in the world, what brings them joy, and how it feels to be in their presence.

Once you know your EBPs, you'll use them as your standard. They will make blessing and releasing the wrong people easier and identifying the right people infinitely clearer. Using your EBPs consistently will change everything in your love life for good. Owning what you want with EBPs is also a feminist act. It's a big "fuck you" to the systems and people who would rather you shrink, be more pleasing and convenient, so as not to disrupt the status quo. In this way, you are revolutionizing your dating life to center yourself, instead of centering the wants of a future partner.

I've seen that EBPs are *the* answer to attracting the best relationship of your life. In the process, you'll be attracting the right courageous opportunities, soul-quenching friendships, and bold-ass boundaries.

Here's how I created EBPs. After my toxic relationship with Dylan ended, I was free of the vicious loop of dating terribleness, and I was also terrified. I had been a matchmaker. I had a bunch of dating skills for other people, but in my own love life I felt like a total beginner. Before meeting Dylan, my dating life wasn't great. I was bumbling around in my dating life in my mid-twenties, feeling constantly behind my friends in established relationships, going on boring dates, and getting let down by repeated situationships. I tried everything. When I was feeling particularly desperate, I created a giant, specific checklist after searching through YouTube at 1 a.m. and taking the advice of a manifesting coach.

I kept this long list in my pocket hoping to find the right person, but it just became a forgotten, crumpled-up piece of paper once I washed it in my jeans at my neighborhood laundromat.

Whenever I became rigid with my dating preferences, I would go on very few dates, nitpick the ones I did go on, and fall into a pit of despair after there was still no spark.

Then I'd swing to the opposite: I'd get super open-minded and look for someone "with a job who was nice." These open-minded preferences were very surface level. After a bunch of bad dates, the fear that someone who met my desires didn't exist was real. But getting super open-minded left too much wiggle room for interpretation. I ended up going on dates that were even more miserable because my preferences were so open. This is why when your friend, coworker, therapist, or mother tries to set you up with someone who meets none of your desired preferences and gives you the advice "You never know! Give them a try! People can surprise you!"—*run*.

Using an open-minded strategy was letting everyone into my dating party who had a pulse. I was cleaning up sticky Solo cups and half-empty Fritos bags after a ton of people who had no business being in my house.

But when I met Dylan, he met this open-minded checklist and stuff from my rigid checklist as well. I thought, *OMG, this is perfect on paper!*

After this relationship proved to be a soul-sucking mess, I was left with thoughts like, *Do I just have a "bad picker"? Can I even trust myself and what I want? Are my preferences too much or not enough? Is what I want even possible?*

I now know that swinging between being really vague and really rigid in my preferences was a trauma response. This is what I call Preferences Underfunctioning and Overfunctioning.

Underfunctioning versus overfunctioning is a distinction made by psychologist Murray Bowen and popularized by Harriet Lerner, PhD, in her book *The Dance of Anger*. It describes these two states of being as a normal, human response to anxiety and past trauma. Either we overfunction by leaning forward, muscling, and trying to control and fix (i.e., taking on super-rigid preferences), or we underfunction by leaning back or not making decisions at all (i.e., having super-open-minded preferences). This pattern of underfunctioning and overfunctioning is like the classic pattern of an older child manically planning and micromanaging their mom's sixtieth birthday party and the youngest child literally just showing up.

Preferences Underfunctioning means you are defaulting to the "You never know! Give them a try!" camp. Underneath the surface you're afraid that what you want is "too much" or that it doesn't truly exist.

Underfunctioning can sound like, "I just want someone nice who has a job," "I'm not really picky, I just want someone who can have a good conversation." If you're thinking, *Well, Lily, I want to be open to being surprised!*, that's like saying, "I want a job and I'll do anything so long as they pay me!" You might land a dream job randomly. Or more than likely you'll end up at a job with a shitty boss, stale breakroom pastries, no perks, and a mediocre paycheck every two weeks.

What's beneath these open-minded statements is that you're not giving yourself permission to actually want (and have) what you want. This negates your agency. You have to actually claim what you want in *detail* if you want to find the right person.

Speaking of claiming preferences in detail…

Preferences Overfunctioning looks like using super-rigid preferences in an attempt to minimize the risk of being with the wrong person, wasting your time, or being disappointed.

This could sound like, "Oh, they don't have a graduate degree? Not the right fit." Or "They seem to spend all their time with family…would they have time for me?" Or "They don't seem to value travel as much as I do. Pass."

Preferences overfunctioning comes with an energy of self-protection, being guarded, and being quick to judge. And for good reason. You've been hurt before and/or witnessed someone you love get hurt. You haven't found what you want, so the response has been to get very specific.

Trudy, a client from my matchmaking days, was the picture of overfunctioning in her preferences. Her checklist was as follows:

> Must be six feet tall or taller, but not over six foot four.

> Went to a top ten U.S. university (if not an Ivy).

> Works out at least five days per week with cardio and rigorous weight training.

> Cooks like Stanley Tucci, but not obsessive about it.

> Must read at least five one-hundred-plus-page books per quarter.

I could feel that underneath the surface of her preferences was a pulsing fear. She had experienced so much disappointment in her dating life that she didn't feel emotionally safe. She was looking around every corner for every single red flag, and she didn't trust herself to never settle again. So she overcorrected by micromanaging her preferences to hopefully avoid future disappointment.

I called her one Thursday with a match who met all these rigid requirements. He was excited to meet her and was open to being set up on that Saturday.

I stepped outside my coworking space in lower Manhattan and I shared the news of this exciting match with her. "He meets all your preferences and is free to go on a date with you this coming Saturday!"

Her response was, "What the fuck is wrong with him that he doesn't already have plans on Saturday?"

The match was dead on arrival.

I took a beat and a deep breath. It took me a second to register that she was being serious. My brain was screaming: "Uhhhhh, ma'am, aren't you *also* free on Saturday? What the fuck do you think is wrong with *you*?"

But instead of giving her that energy (I definitely would have gotten fired!), I gave her the company line about "giving people a chance" and staying open to dates being information-gathering experiences.

She went on the date. It did not go well. Because "good on paper" matches rarely feel good IRL.

That's why neither a rigid checklist nor a pile of open-minded mush works to attract your person. I want to invite you to the juicy middle between over- and underfunctioning—the land of Essence-Based Preferences.

EBPs go spelunking way beneath the surface of a two-dimensional checklist.

Defining and embracing my EBPs is what took me from oscillating between "good on paper" matches that went up in a vicious cycle of bad dates and situationships to attracting the love of my life (someone I wouldn't have chosen with my original "checklist").

It's now time to write yourself a massive permission slip so that you can get *exactly* what you want. Let's get going.

STEP ONE: DEFINE THE LOGISTICS

Defining the logistics means knowing the on-paper, measurable stuff you want, like age, height, and education preferences, but with an Essence-Based Preferences flavor.

This means not only asking yourself what age range you want but digging deeper and asking yourself *why* you want that preference and how you hope someone within that age range makes you feel. Do this for **Every. Single. Preference.** This is so that you can (a) want what you want and (b) be open to being surprised by the right person who fits how you want to feel.

It might sound annoying to answer all these questions, but this clarity will lead to dates that actually are in line with how you want to feel. Your preferences are that important.

Here's an example. If you want someone who is five eleven or taller—that's great, list it. You get to want what you want! And then also ask yourself: How do I hope to *feel* with someone who is five eleven or taller?

Usually, my clients say something like, "I want to be attracted, and I'm attracted to taller people. I want them to have confidence, and when they walk into a room, I want to take notice."

I can see right through that answer to the Essence-Based Preferences angle underneath, which is that you don't just want someone "confident." You want someone who is warm, affectionate, present, attractive to you (obvi), and connective (because of how they enter a room). See how much deeper that is than just "five eleven"?

The other magical thing about Logistical Preferences with the EBP flavor is that the right person might (and probably will) surprise you. They might be hot as hell, confident, *and* "only" five eight. If the person is confident as hell, affectionate, gives the best hugs, holds eye contact in a way that makes you feel truly seen… then maybe for that awesome a person they could be five eight and you'd be super attracted. Attraction is not limited to what we can describe on paper. The EBP process gives you the language to be specific *and* open to the right people.

This isn't open-mindedness for the sake of being open. By knowing how you want to feel, you can measure every date and know you're getting exactly what you want without settling.

For me, it's all about the ponytail example. One of my clients, Emma, was *sure* that she wanted a guy with a "man bun" (in other words, a man with long hair; it was one of her nonnegotiables for attraction).

I saw that this Logistical Preference was something deeper

than just hair, so I asked her, "How do you hope to feel with someone with a man bun?"

Turns out, Emma had met a lot of dudes with man buns who were creative, OK with bucking gender norms, progressive, intelligent, and funny. And after really shitty experiences with other kinds of men in her dating life, she was clinging to the man buns for dear life. So her brain did what brains do. It made up a story that a man bun was the surefire sign that someone had the qualities she wanted.

After doing this exercise, she could identify that she wanted to be attracted, and that she wanted her date's external vibe to express his creativity.

With Logistical Preferences, we start at the surface, then go deeper. Take my client Rebecca's preferences for education. In our session, she described that she wanted the Logistical Preference for all her dates to have a graduate degree. Her first response to my "How do you want to feel with this preference?" was a little basic. I could tell she was holding back when she said, "I want them to value education. I went to school for a long time and want them to understand that choice."

I told her to go deeper, and I asked, "Where do you think that answer comes from?" She took a beat, then a lightbulb went on. She said, "My dad wanted all his kids to get a higher education. I'm afraid that if I choose someone who didn't choose that life, they won't get me or my dad won't approve."

And then I said, "Giving your dad back his stuff, only listening to yourself, how do *you* want to feel with this education preference?"

She took a deep breath and responded, "I want to feel understood. I want to feel really deeply connected. I want to feel belonging. I want to feel intellectually matched and excited by our conversations."

WHOOMP! THERE IT IS.

Rebecca now knew that while a graduate degree was a "nice to have," it wasn't a deal-breaker. Instead she would measure whether or not she felt intellectually met and seen.

Everyone's dating advice and preferences are a reflection of their own learned safety and coping mechanisms, biases, and unique desires. Rebecca's dad pushing graduate degrees as a sign of success was a reflection of his own experiences and internal narratives. Through this process, you're going to realize just how much you've inherited from other people in your preferences. These could be people who you thought knew more than you because they're in a relationship.

The secret that I'm thrilled to let you in on is this: No one knows what you want and need more than you. You are the expert of what you want. And with EBPs, you'll be the expert on how to find it.

When you know how you want to feel in the right relationship, you can allow the right person to surprise you in how they show up in the world. Because as it turns out, as Rebecca started dating with this EBP process, she met someone awesome. He *didn't* have a graduate degree—*and* he was superintellectual, he was intelligent, and he respected the hell out of her commitment to get a higher education. But he didn't even have a college degree. He was just an out-of-this-world-smart computer programmer who got a job at a top tech firm out of high school. With this process,

Rebecca knew how she wanted to feel with each of her EBPs, so she could measure it every step of the way.

> ### The patriarchy has impacted your preferences.

We all have been impacted by our environment (duh), which means you might have some preferences rooted in old patriarchal conditioning that need to be unpacked. To cleanse your EBPs of preferences that aren't in alignment with your feminist values, ask yourself questions like, "Where did this preference come from? Is this mine, or does it belong to someone who taught it to me?" Maybe it actually belongs to a parent, friend, or coworker, in which case give it back to them. You're reimagining what you want on your terms, not based on anyone else's expectations.

STEP TWO: WHAT VALUES AND PERSONALITY TRAITS DO YOU WANT?

This is my favorite part of the EBP process. It's like the chocolatey center of the Tootsie Pop. It's the gazebo in the Stars Hollow town square. It's the center of your new dating strategy and is where everything comes together. In addition to the preferences you can measure on a résumé, that is, Logistical Preferences, we need to unpack the deeper, less on-paper-quantifiable stuff too. Once you understand the values and personality traits you desire for your ideal partner, you can see them better with an EBP lens.

On the surface, everyone wants the same thing: kind, funny, and smart. And everyone has a basic definition of each of those desired traits. But when you get down to the EBP level, you'll see that *your* version, your definition of "kind, funny, smart," is distinct from everyone else's on this planet.

First, let's unpack the difference between personality traits and values.

Personality traits are how a person shows up in the world. (For example, is this person outgoing, kind, generous, compassionate, worldly, or intelligent?)

Values are a person's underpinning beliefs that influence how they show up in the world. (For example, is this person family oriented and/or committed to social justice?)

In this process, you're going to brain dump every single personality trait and value you want onto a sheet of paper. Give yourself massive permission to take up space on the page.

From there, the intention is to create three to five EBP root words and phrases that beautifully, clearly describe the personality traits and values of your ideal person.

Afterward you'll have your own unique definition of each word tailored to what makes you come alive across the table.

To find your living, breathing definition of each of your preferences, you'll ask yourself the following three questions:

1. What does this word mean to you?
2. What does someone who is _____ value?
3. How do you hope to feel in the presence of someone who is _____?

Here's an example: My client Alison shared that she wanted someone "worldly."

When we met, she was in her mid-thirties, was in a vicious cycle of mediocre dates, and had never been in a fulfilling relationship. She was ready to take control of her dating destiny, so we immediately dove into creating all her Essence-Based Preferences.

At first, when asked what "worldly" meant to her, she said, "That means they're well traveled and care about the world."

Then I asked her to go deeper.

Here's what she came up with:

From Alison's perspective, a person who is "worldly" is someone really curious about different cultures and who has traveled a lot internationally to places where they didn't speak the language. They care about climate change and the refugee crisis happening around the world. They can have a conversation with different types of people easily. They are bilingual or have always wanted to learn another language. They are progressive in their politics. They identify as a feminist. They read books written by a diverse group of authors. They are always learning and are passionate about people.

In terms of "what they value," to her, this kind of person would value learning, a growth mindset, the well-being of others, their ability to travel, and their financial health. They value feeling grounded and taking care of themselves and others.

For "How do you want someone with this preference to make you feel?" Alison knew the answer immediately. She wanted to feel understood, joined by their passion, cared for, and inspired daily.

See how much deeper we got? Essence-Based Preferences go beyond the basic to exactly what *you* want and how you want to feel. And yes, my clients sometimes get annoyed by how many times in this process I ask, "What does that mean to you? Go deeper. Now, what does that mean to you?" Beneath that deeper self-inquiry is the answer to attracting the right partner.

When Alison had gone through all her Essence-Based Preferences with these questions and this intentional lens, she had a clear, joyful, unique understanding of her future relationship that felt exciting and alive. Defining her EBPs made what she wanted feel closer. The more you know about what you want and the more you can ask for it, the more likely you are to attract what you want to you.

Her preferences weren't a rigid wall or an open-minded pile of mush. They were an impressionist painting that felt real and that she could use as a metric to decide whether future conversations and dates were right or wrong for her.

Defining her EBPs had a life-changing impact on Alison. She was finally centering herself and her needs. And living in a patriarchal society, she hadn't been taught to prioritize her needs, especially in her love life. But now with EBPs, she's putting her needs first, not wasting her time, and finally trusting what she wants.

It doesn't matter if her future partner reads every book that she does. It just matters that they care about the world in a way similar to how Alison does. Essence-Based Preferences are a radical invitation to center yourself and how you want to feel as *the* answer to attracting what you want. Once she knew how she wanted to feel with her preferences, she knew the exact steps forward to attracting what she wanted.

Your Essence-Based Preference root words and definitions

will make it so much easier to talk about what you want. It will make it easier to share with friends who want to set you up.

I hear you in my ear again, and you're saying, "Lily, why do I need to answer so many questions? Can't this just be a normal dating book where I speed through the chapters and feel like I got something out of it and then forget everything I learned?"

Nope, I don't want just a surface-level anything for you after reading this book. I want to help you get epic results, and intentional effort leads to intentional results. You have to ask yourself these questions about every single preference to get to the essence of what you want.

STEP THREE: NARROWING DOWN YOUR EBP ROOT WORDS

This process was inspired by Brené Brown's book *Dare to Lead*. In this book, she shares dozens of values and says that in her research, people only had two to three root values from which every behavior and belief flowed. Yes, narrowing down your values is hard work—*and* knowing your precise values will help you navigate the world with more agency and power.

Narrowing down your EBP root words and phrases will also be hard—*and* they will help you navigate the murky, weird-ass world of dating with clarity and prowess.

After you brain dump all the personality traits and values you want in a future partner, ask yourself for each word, "Is this word the *root* of what I want? Or does it *describe* what I want?" To get going, you can circle the words that keep coming up multiple times. These are your clues to get to the root.

My client Sherry said she wanted someone observant, attentive, funny, and compassionate. When she reflected on what the *root* was, she realized that the word "compassionate" was at the center. The way she saw compassion being expressed was in seeing how observant they were, recognizing their desire to want to make people feel at home, being attentive to people's stories and shares, and asking good follow-up questions. Her root Essence-Based Preference became "compassionate connector."

If you're stuck with a vague, surface-level list and are asking yourself, "What do I even want? I don't know!," be willing to ask yourself some deeper questions, and don't be afraid to play on paper.

For instance, if the word that repeatedly comes up for you is "kind," but you don't know what that looks like in a partner, ask yourself questions such as:

> What does kindness look like for me in the real world?
>
> What was the kindest moment I've ever experienced in my life?
>
> What was a moment where I really felt joined by a close friend, past partner, or family member and I really felt embraced in their kindness?

Mine your past experience for the data you need to flesh out your Essence-Based Preference.

If one of your phrases is "emotional intelligence," you can ask yourself questions such as: Have they gone to therapy? What do their friendships look like? What do they read in their spare time?

Asking yourself all these questions will help you brain dump exactly what you want on paper, both determining the definition of your Essence-Based Preferences and helping you to clarify your root words.

STEP FOUR: WAVE GOODBYE TO THE "SHOULDS"

Once you go through your Logistical Preferences, personality traits, and values with an Essence-Based Preferences lens, it's time to comb through your desires to get rid of *all* the "shoulds."

The word "should" is not helpful. Ever. "Shoulds" usually come in the form of someone else telling you what is or is not acceptable. "Shoulding" is often rooted in shame, with statements such as "You should want someone who got a degree from a prestigious university," or "You should want to be with someone who makes more money than you." Look out for any sneaky patriarchal conditioning that might be present in these "shoulds" as well.

Look through your preferences and circle anything with "should" energy. Where did that story originate? Maybe from your mom telling you from a young age that you "should" want a certain preference or quality. Maybe it's your coworker telling you only suckers date people who make less money than them. Perfectionism says, "You should know everything about your preferences already," or "You should have met your partner already."

These "should" thoughts are the result of perfectionism trying to keep you safe from rejection and the unknown. These forces are also keeping you majorly stuck in your dating life. That's why you have to shed perfectionism and take messy action to find love.

> ## You literally can't do this wrong.

You can't fuck this up by wanting too much. The cool part about EBPs is that they will grow and change. Remember, it's a living, breathing document. It is meant to expand as you learn more about what you want and need.

When you hear the perfectionistic "shoulding" voice come up in this process, know that she's trying to keep you safe from the vulnerability and potential rejection that come with opening up to more. You get to feel compassion for that part of yourself that wants certainty.

Then you get to remind yourself that you are expanding into more. Your love life doesn't require perfection; it requires presence. You don't have to know every single preference or do this perfectly to still be on the right path.

This process is an unhurried unfolding.

Don't freak out. You are exactly where you need to be. Get started now, and keep this preferences work close as you move through this book.

THE POWER OF "BOTH/AND"

You may think that someone this awesome doesn't exist because you haven't met them yet. This is a normal fear. To combat that thought error ('cause that's what it is), I want to teach you *the* tool I use every single day.

"Should" (as most "shoulds" are) is rooted in an either/or binary, such as, *"Either* I find someone with a 'strong personality' who can be with me and I need to be submissive, *or* I will be alone forever because it's too hard to find that needle-in-a-haystack person."

Instead of being trapped in those limiting options, "both/and" is the salve that sounds like this:

> *"Both* I'm nervous about these preferences—*and* I'm willing to try."

> *"Both* I was taught to want less—*and* I'm unlearning a bunch of shit that doesn't serve my love life right now."

> *"Both* I get to expand into a different vision for my love life—*and* maybe it will be hard to find someone awesome, *and* I do hard things all the time."

"Both/and" is like being in a luxurious, gleaming airport hangar. (I'm specifically thinking about the iconic one from the movie *Crazy Rich Asians.*) It's so big and gorgeous, and it has a giant door where you can see the whole sky. This magical "both/and" airport hangar just expands for whatever you want to hold. You get to take up all the space you want. You also can bless and release the "shoulds" and "either/ors" that aren't serving the expansiveness of what you desire.

By claiming your Essence-Based Preferences, you're not only getting clear on what you want; you're creating a dating life that is boundaried as fuck. When you know how you want to feel with the right person, you are more likely to find them. You're less likely to settle. You're more likely to bless and release people who are wrong for you. You're taking charge of your love life. And it will pay off.

I hear your voice in the back of my head saying, "Lily, you say I get to want what I want, but what if I have such a specific view of what I'm looking for that I reject the *right* person?!"

I totally get it, and this is why I have you note how you want to *feel* with each preference. These preferences aren't meant to be a wall that you build up to keep all the plebeians out. Instead, you get to measure how you feel as an indicator if someone is right for you or not.

When you tune in to how you want to feel, instead of clinging to a particular word or checklist, you will end up in the right relationship. Of course you get to want exactly what you want—*and* you get to be open to being surprised by what shape your person comes in. I can pretty much guarantee that they will surprise you. And you can trust that how you want to feel will guide you into the right relationship, no matter what.

Bottom line: You get to trust your body and how you feel.

If you have any resistance in this process, let me give you a shot of hope—

Before diving into her Essence-Based Preferences, my client Debbie said, "Lily, this feels pointless. Why even try when I haven't met a person with these traits?"

When she asked this question, I could see her body was tense. Her face looked super concerned. I saw that the stakes were high.

Debbie had tried everything in her dating life, and nothing else had worked. Her urgency in this moment reflected something deeper—she feared that what she wanted wasn't possible. Debbie started to believe that she'd "just die alone anyway." She had already decided that this process wasn't going to work, which is very natural. Our brains want to protect us from vulnerability at all costs.

Your brain has made a story of those experiences to protect you from future rejection. And so the first thing that I would recommend that you do is practice a massive amount of self-compassion.

It's not necessary to believe that someone exists right now who meets all these Essence-Based Preferences. The point is that you get to believe yourself.

GET INTO THE ENERGY OF WHAT YOU WANT

If you're feeling confused or stuck on your EBPs, here's a journaling meditation to get unstuck and into the energy of what you want. Read through these prompts and then give yourself all the time you need to write down what comes up for you. If your EBPs are still unclear after this first go-round, give yourself permission to get messy on the page. This process of defining and refining your EBPs will take time. Give yourself the grace to take on this meditation as many times as you want.

Take three deep breaths. Breathe in for five, hold for three, and exhale for ten.

Check in with your body. Is there any tension anywhere?

Breathe into it. Release what you can.

Give yourself some compassion. You can touch your belly or heart and choose to let the tension go for this moment.

Imagine that you are walking into a third date with someone you're really excited to see again.

You walk into the restaurant, and your date stands to greet you. You hug.

Imagine what it feels like to hug this person. Then you sit down and you have the best and most connected date of your life. In this moment, you know that this is different.

And now that we've set the stage for this different sort of date, I want you to imagine what you talk about. What comes up? What are they interested in? What makes you both come alive in this moment?

How does it feel to be in their presence?

They just said the sexiest, most attractive thing you've ever heard. What did they say? How do you feel at that moment?

You're about to leave the date. And before you do, you look at them on this third date and appreciate something about them. What do you appreciate?

Then I want you to turn your attention to yourself. What do you appreciate about yourself on this date? Give yourself some credit.

You and your amazing date stand up and leave the restaurant (you're definitely going to kiss outside).

How did it feel to be in the energy of this date? In your journal, write out what came up for you.

What did you notice?

This is what it's like to be in the energy of your YES and what you desire. This is what it's like to listen to your body and take her desires seriously.

When I was single, I used this visualization to get crystal clear on my EBPs. Here's what I came up with for myself:

> **Joyful as hell:** Has a blast wherever they go, great friendships, prioritizes laughter, and creative in the way they move through the world. Will dance or sing at the drop of a hat. I wanted to feel held, seen, and celebrated.

> **Resilient:** Been through some shit, has grown from it, reflective, grateful for the learnings and growth, holds the "both/and" of hard stuff and joyful stuff, powerful, wise. I wanted to feel like we were growing and moving forward together.

> **Compassionately generous:** Prioritizes people in their life, gives what they can, goes and sits next to the person at the table who is alone, and is passionate about making the world a kinder place. They're excited to be generous and present in a romantic partnership. I wanted to feel belonging and joined in my passion and fierceness for others.

After I did this work, I felt clear on what I wanted and how I wanted to feel in the right relationship. I used this information to choose dates that fit my EBPs, and when I felt hopeless, I went out in to the world looking for slivers of evidence that my EBPs existed in the real world. When I saw them, I said a hearty and grateful, "Thank You, More Please!" to build evidence that what I wanted was possible (a process I teach you more in chapter 8). Then, I felt sure that when the right relationship came, I'd know it because of how well I knew my own desires. I knew when I met my future husband, Chris, and we went on our first date, I felt how I wanted to feel. This is how I ended up knowing he was the human I wanted to build a life with. You've got this, and it's just the beginning.

MESSY HOMEWORK: Digging into Your EBPs

Put on some music that makes you feel like a badass and follow the prompts below. Remember, messy progress is better than no action. Get going.

1. List your Logistical Preferences (in other words, stuff that can be measured on paper):
   - Age range
   - Height range
   - Preferred body types
   - Preferred locations
   - Desire to have children
   - Preferred religions (if any)
   - Preferred education level
   - Preferred career types
   - Ideal interests
   - Preferred money habits (How do they treat money?)
   - Your deal-breakers and why

2. Go deeper. Ask yourself the following questions for each Logistical Preference—
   - Why do I want this Logistical Preference? (Example: I want someone in this age range because I want to feel understood and met in the same place in life.)
   - How do I want to feel with this preference?

DISCOVER YOUR PREFERRED PERSONALITY TRAITS AND VALUES

List *every* personality trait and value you want below. Even if it feels like, "Oh shit, I want 'too much,'" there's no such thing. Let yourself go wild on the page. You can ask yourself questions such as:

1. What personality traits do you want your future partner to have?
2. What values do you want your future partner to have?

For every single personality trait and value, ask yourself,

1. What does this word mean to me?
2. What does a person who is _____ care about?
3. How do you hope to feel in the presence of someone who is _____?

Then narrow your list down to three to five root words that summarize the big themes in the personality traits and values you want. From there, you can create your own unique definition for those words and phrases. Once you have defined them, these words and phrases will become your living, breathing definition.

Here are some amazing client examples of Essence-Based Preferences to get you inspired—

Empathetic connector: Someone who connects to themselves and others deeply, freely, and affectionately. Aware of themselves and their biases, working on it all in therapy. Lives their feminist values with openness, warmth, and curiosity toward themselves and others.

Enthusiastic nerd: Passionately curious about the world and people in it, always exploring and learning new things. Will follow their passion to go on trips, into new friendships, and deep conversations. Always seeking out joy in their hobbies, work, and day-to-day life.

Grounded confidence: Self-assured and confident in themselves and in their partner. Financially secure and skilled in self-sufficiency and personal well-being. Committed to mutual growth, both as individuals and in our shared journey as partners.

Look around your life for people who meet your EBPs right now, and say "Thank you, more please!" to build evidence that what you want exists right now. You've got this. Let's go!

5

Become Your Own Matchmaker: You Have to Be Picky, Y'all

"What's bringing you joy lately?"

She stopped in her tracks, made direct eye contact, and said, "Whoa, I have to go onstage in a moment, but I want to find you afterward to have this conversation."

Damn, I thought, *I've got juice.*

I was chatting with a well-known journalist at the *Gilmore Girls* Fan Fest (aka GG Fest), and I was a then matchmaker, at the very beginning of creating my coaching company, Date Brazen.

This question is my favorite of all time for two reasons—

1. It lets people know right away that I am a person who cares deeply about you and what brings you joy.

2. It also shows me who the other person is. Are they game to get real in a conversation quickly? Do they know what brings them joy? Are they willing to ask themselves this question?

After her panel moderation, this journalist came and found me in the sea of people at the GG Fest. She answered that question, saying playing with her nephews last week during her time off was bringing her all the joy.

Then she asked me the same question.

My answer was my new business, Date Brazen, where I get to help women around the world thrive in their dating lives (you know I had to plug it).

This question has changed my life.

This question is what I call a Qualifying/Disqualifying Question (Q/D Question). I have hundreds of them. They were compiled while I was setting up a ton of dates as a top professional matchmaker. We're going to use them to help you become your *own* feminist-as-hell matchmaker. These questions will get you in the driver's seat of finding out if someone is the right fit for you in less time than you knew was possible.

This "What's bringing you joy?" question meant that I was memorable and connective. Just like in this very professional *Gilmore Girls* networking scenario, these Q/D questions will set you apart to the *right* people in your dating life. Asking these questions will also mean receiving an answer. One of the most powerful ways to free yourself from soul-sucking, time-wasting conversations with the wrong people is to listen to the answer. As

Dr. Maya Angelou put so beautifully, "When someone shows you who they are, believe them the first time."

They will set you free from boring conversations or never-ending pen pal conversations with people you will never meet. There is nothing I hate more than a "nowhere" conversation.

"How was your weekend? What a cute dog! That looks like a fun trip!" Barf.

Social convention says to keep it light in the first conversation with a potential date. And we are about throwing social convention TO THE FUCKING WIND.

You're here to find the right person for you with more joy in the process. You are not here to have a zillion surface-level conversations about the weather or your weekend plans. Nor is it your goal go on a bajillion first, second, or third dates with folks that you have zero in common with.

You're reading this book and investing in your dating life because you want to find something real, soul-quenching, and so reciprocal, sexy, and full of laughter that it feels extraordinary. This is your invitation to say what you want and be beautifully intense about it. That's what these Q/D Questions are here to help you with.

I can tell you right now that I know you're selling yourself short if you're not using Qualifying/Disqualifying Questions. You're not being picky enough with the people you're on dates with (or at least not powerfully picky enough). And I know that amid all this, there is fear.

My hypothesis is that you've struggled with the fear of saying the wrong thing. You've responded by trying to be the one for everyone or by giving most people a chance. It ends up attracting no one or the wrong people to you. Maybe you're struggling with a belief that "my picker is broken." Maybe you don't trust your own ability to gauge whether or not someone is a good date.

This stuff is tough. Dating is a microcosm of every hope, dream, fear, insecurity, and desire that we have as humans. It deeply matters to your overall well-being. I repeat this often because it's easy to forget.

There's that dirty social convention that says that it is frivolous to care so much about your dating life. And there are the beliefs that "it will just happen when you least expect it," or "try less and it will come to you!" You were most likely taught that your desire stinks up a date and people can smell it and will stay away. Or worst of all, you believe that you are somehow deeply flawed and *that's* why you're still single.

These narratives are deeply harmful and sexist. They are telling women that having desires makes them less desirable. It's an obvious recipe for women to shrink who they are and what they want.

This chapter is calling you to the mat to finally take up your space, ask for what you want with boldness, and ask questions that allow others to see you and allow them to show you who they are.

THE QUESTIONS YOU HAVE BEEN WAITING FOR

The answer to finding more is using these Qualifying/Disqualifying Questions in every moment of your dating life. In a few short pages, you're going to be able to build a list of juicy questions that will help you know exactly who to keep talking to, ask out, and bless and release immediately.

Here's how I created this magical system.

As a top professional matchmaker, I had thousands of calls with potential matches for my clients, and I created this system to sort through the masses with intention. Honestly, there were too many people, and this is one of the reasons I know someone awesome is out there for you. There are just so many humans that you haven't met yet, in your city, who are single, or who are about to be single right now.

The E! True Hollywood Story of finding dates for my match-making clients went a little something like this: We have a data-base the company has built. Our job is to fill the database with single people (mostly straight, cis men) from literally everywhere we go. Then we set them all up on dates with our clients. This isn't the case with every matchmaking service, though with the one I was working at, women dating men made up the majority of the clientele.

I'd be at a restaurant, and there'd be a cute guy at the neighboring booth. I would go straight up to him and say some version of, "Hey, so you're adorable, and I'm a matchmaker. Want to be set up?"

I once went to a friend's party, brought my computer, and signed up every single available man there into this database. Chris, my future husband, was one of them. I got thirty dollars per sign-up and each gentleman would get a payout in the form of a date.

I was on every dating app and dating site for my company. All with the paid upgrades, which is how I know that those are trash, something I'll cover in chapter 6. My job was to basically catfish men into talking to me, tell them I was a matchmaker, and then get on the phone to see if they were a good match for my clients.

I made more than a thousand calls with potential dates for my clients over the course of three years. After the first year of setting up some pretty terrible dates, I came up with my Q/D Questions system to gauge within the first five minutes whether or not this person would be a good fit. My success rate of good matches skyrocketed. "Success" to this matchmaking firm was based on whether they wanted to go on a second date.

When you employ this system on your own, with your own agency and gut instinct, you will find success that far exceeds just getting a second date. Let me give you an example of this Q/D system in matchmaking action.

My client wanted to find someone funny and who shared her witty, intelligent humor (think Christopher Guest's *Waiting for Guffman*). She also was a feminist and wanted someone who shared those same values. On an Essence-Based Preferences level, she wanted to feel belonging, emotional safety, and shared knowing. For her, this would be measured in their ability to laugh easily with a date. To screen matches for her, I would ask potential dates the following Q/D Question. "What's made you laugh hardest lately?"

Some men responded with, "I'm always rewatching *The Office*, which still makes me laugh. And my family, they're pretty hilarious too. We hung out last weekend, and my brother blah blah blah…" (honestly, that's where my mind would go after hundreds of these calls).

OK, so he's into mockumentaries, he's smart, he's a little bit sarcastic, and he enjoys some edgy humor. Check. And he is family oriented (at least a little bit). Check. But some of these conversations turned into nightmare scenarios, where I knew immediately that this person needed to be taken out of the dating pool and thrust into a therapy session.

With one such gentleman, let's call him Craig, I asked the "What's made you laugh hardest lately?" question. He thought for a minute and said, "I was on a boat with my buddies and my son this weekend, and a boat full of fat women drove by. They all had bikinis on, and I said to everyone, 'Baby got back?' They all died laughing."

I wanted to vomit. What a problematic jerk.

With this simple, non-leading question, this man revealed to me, basically a stranger, that not only was he fatphobic, he was also unkind, aloof, and apparently teaching his son to behave this way, too! His sense of humor could be categorized as "objectifying and debasing women," so he obviously didn't share my client's feminist values. He was a big no for her (and generally a big no for the betterment of humankind). Unfortunately, this kind of situation happened a lot.

As a curvy woman, I used to feel a lot of shame about my size and desirability. This shame was internalized from years of watching plus-size women on TV only play the "best friend," hearing my family members criticize their own bodies, going to WeightWatchers meetings at age fourteen, and eating up the SlimFast-generation bullshit.

Many times, these matchmaking conversations with men

made me doubt that what I wanted was possible. I thought that it wasn't in the cards for me to be loved as I was. If this story triggered you, or if it feels like it confirmed what you fear is true of all men or people who are single and available (i.e., "There are no single people who are kind, and this story is just kindling on that fire"), I encourage you to be mindful. Your experience has probably given you a lot of "evidence that what you want is not possible."

There are going to be a hell of a lot of people who are wrong for you—and that's a good thing.

> **You are for the few, not the many.**

This truth occurred to me when trying to build my business. I was listening to a podcast with marketing genius Seth Godin. He was talking about how business owners usually are trying to talk to too many people at once, hence talking to no one. And why are we talking to too many people at once? Because of the fear that we will attract no one. So we cast a wide net.

Sound familiar?

I was doing this in the very early days of Date Brazen—"Come talk to me if you're a human who is single! *Please?*"

I felt desperate, just like I had in my dating life. In my first year of trying this strategy, I had one client. (Thank God she was a freaking awesome human being.) Then I heard Seth, this brilliant, bald, bespectacled man, talking about something called "minimum viable audience," and my life changed.

Instead of trying to be for everyone, Seth said the answer to incredible business is to define the smallest number of people who are right for you and dedicate all your energy and time to talking to them.

I got to be picky, y'all! I no longer was speaking to every single person in the universe. I was talking specifically to single women who identify as intersectional feminists. I focused on single women who wanted to buck patriarchal dating culture, know that they are whole with or without a relationship, and desired to find love, experience joy, and live courageously in the process.

My business doubled that year—and I finally had language to describe why Qualifying/Disqualifying Questions were so freaking powerful.

They are an expression of your "minimum viable audience" (i.e., your Essence-Based Preferences). They get you talking to the *right* people for you. Again, you are for the few—not the many.

With this process, the people who ghost you, don't want to go on another date, or have shitty answers to your Q/D Question automatically disqualify themselves from your minimum viable audience (i.e., your few).

This is good news because in this new way of thinking about your dating pool, there are just too many people out there for you to meaningfully engage with every single one.

If you're struggling with this concept and thinking, *I don't want to disqualify the wrong person*, think about it this way. You go to a warehouse party in Brooklyn (not my scene after an ill-fated paint cannon to my face years ago, but I digress). It's *full* of eligible single people whom you might be interested in. Like, thousands of them.

When you walk into this party, you instinctively will know

that you can only talk to 1 to 2 percent of them before getting exhausted and needing to go home. Your brilliant body and brain will pick up on who you want to dive into conversation with, based on your attraction, how they talk, and how they treat the people around them.

After you ask someone a question, you will know by the way they answer whether or not you want to continue the conversation. This is the power of "minimum viable audience" and your Q/D Questions.

To my friends with a little anxiety still in their chests about saying no to the "right person," here's what I know to be true—

If you say no to the "right person" for you, they will enter your life in some other way or you'll meet another "right person" for you. You'll bump into them at a coffee shop. You'll run into them on a dating app. Your friend will introduce you, and your brilliant love story will commence.

Side note: I don't believe in "the one." I believe that there are many people who are awesome for you whom you could choose to love. I say this as a person who is happily married to the most awesome human. Chris and I marvel at how we met, get to choose each other daily, and love being together. *Both/and* if we had never been introduced, I'm pretty sure we both would have met other people and had different love stories.

Getting anxious about saying no to "the one" is diminishing your agency. It's saying that your happiness and your connection can only be possible in a very small window with one very specific person. I believe there is too much magic and spaciousness in the world for that to be the truth.

THANK YOU, MORE PLEASE

The magic of Q/D Questions isn't in expecting or hoping for a rigid, specific answer in response. It's in seeing how they interpret the question and how they respond.

If you're looking for someone who finds joy in their everyday life and you ask, "What's bringing you joy right now?" and they say, "Nothing." Then, boom! You know that this person is not for you. Wish them well and release them.

If you ask the same question and someone responds with, "I just went on this amazing hike!" or "You know, work has been pretty tough lately, but I've loved going climbing afterward" or "I've been rewatching *Parks and Recreation* lately and, my god, is that a great show," then you know that person is someone who:

1. Knows what brings them joy,
2. Is ready to respond to a deeper question, and
3. Meets your preference, at least at a Level 1.

Yes, there are levels to this. You can only know someone so well after texting, a phone call, or even one date. I like to think of getting to know a new potential suitor as Level 1, 2, 3, and higher.

Someone giving the *perfect* response to your Q/D Question when you first meet them does not automatically mean that they are your life partner. You simply have Level 1 knowledge that they meet your preferences. Now it's time to get to Level 2, 3, and 4 knowledge—a first date, going on an adventure together, or eventually meeting their friends.

Beware of good "on paper" matches and answers that don't feel good in person. That's why it's so important to keep asking questions, following your intrigue, and getting more levels of information in different forms of communication.

Below is a list of my Qualifying/Disqualifying Questions, organized by the Essence-Based Preferences I believe they correspond with. They can be mixed and matched. Because I believe you can't say the wrong thing to the right person, you can use any of these at any point! Just make sure the ones you choose deeply resonate with *you*.

ADVENTUROUS QUESTIONS:

- Where's your next big trip taking you?
- What is your favorite part about traveling?
- What trip or adventure are you most grateful you took/went on?

Word of warning: When gauging "adventurous," be aware of surface-level travel conversation. Travel can be a sand-trap conversation topic and keep you stuck on the surface. Try to go deeper.

"ARE THEY A FEMINIST" QUESTIONS:

- What leaders are you inspired by and why?
- What have you been reading lately?
- If you had a million dollars to donate, what causes would you give to?

"Do They Want a Relationship?" Questions:

- What are you looking for in your dating life?
- What do you hope to get out of your dating life?
- What do you hope your life looks like in a few years?
- What are you excited to create in your life this year?

Family-Oriented Questions:

- Who in your family makes you laugh the hardest?
- What's bringing you joy right now? (This gives them a chance to talk about their connections in their life if that brings them joy.)
- What's your favorite part of the holidays?

Financial Independence Questions:

- What are your goals/desires for this year?
- What sort of trips do you love to go on?
- What are you creating in your life this year?
- What do you love spending money on?

Growth Mindset Questions:

- What's your favorite thing about yourself?

- What are you working on in your life?
- What's the best advice you've received lately?
- What's your favorite book recommendation?
- Who's inspiring you most lately?
- What's your favorite self-care activity?
- What's a goal you've reached in the past year you're proud of?

INTELLIGENT/CURIOUS QUESTIONS:

- What have you learned lately that you're really excited about?
- What's your ideal Saturday?
- What sets your heart on fire? (In a good way!)
- What do you like about yourself?
- What's an off-the-beaten-path thing you love to do in the city?
- What could you talk about for hours?

OPEN-MINDED QUESTIONS:

- What have you learned lately that you're really excited about?
- What's your favorite unpopular opinion?
- What are you working on in your life?
- What could you talk about for hours?

OPTIMISTIC QUESTIONS:

- What's bringing you joy lately?
- What's made you laugh the hardest lately?
- What are you looking forward to this week/year?
- What makes you feel hopeful?

OUTGOING QUESTIONS:

- What's bringing you joy right now?
- What do you do for fun?
- Who's inspiring you these days?
- How do you refill your energy tank?

SELF-AWARE QUESTIONS:

- Who are you in your friend group (the planner, the funny one, etc.)?
- What are you working on in your life?
- What's bringing you joy right now?
- What does balance mean to you?
- What do you admire most in a person?

Choosing three to five of these Q/D Questions gives you the framework to know whether or not someone meets your Essence-Based Preferences. This way you'll vet people quickly and not waste any of your time with the wrong people for you. These questions will help you not get so lost in the flurry of a new connection that you abandon your EBPs. A new connection still gets to be fun and flirty and spontaneous. *And* you also get to ask important questions like, "What are you hoping to find in your dating life?" to know if someone is right for you (or not!) and to save yourself massive amounts of heart time and energy.

Some of these Q/D Questions are very direct and pretty intense. You don't have to use the ones you don't like. Release the fear of saying the wrong thing to the right person. Don't be afraid of being "too much" to the right person. Remember, they are also looking for you!

MESSY HOMEWORK: Choose Your Qualifying and Disqualifying Questions

To choose the right Q/D Questions for you, look at your Essence-Based Preferences from chapter 4. Then ask yourself which of these Q/D Questions would help you identify if someone has the preference you desire. What is your version of an ideal answer?

These questions will be the basis of your new online strategy, your messaging strategy, your future boundaries, and your in-person dating strategy.

Circle your favorite Q/D Questions and narrow them down to your favorite three to five! Put them somewhere you'll remember them, like a sticky note on your fridge or a note on your phone. Start asking people in your life these questions to get practice. And when you hear an answer that meets your Essence-Based Preferences, say "Thank you, more please!" This is gathering evidence that you get to have what you want and that what you want exists.

You've got this! Now, get messy and get going.

6

The Wild, Wild West of Online Dating

I hate all dating apps equally. They are a toxic invention of tech bros that gaslight you into thinking that "love is just one swipe away." They convince you that dating just sucks until you meet the right person, which will happen any minute if you are spending every minute on the app!

A dating app also isn't a super-chill and easy place to be a woman, queer, or trans. It can be a chaotic playground of misogynistic, racist, homophobic, transphobic behavior. There isn't data available on how many people have received unsolicited dick pics, but I know the number is high from friends, clients, and even my own personal experience.

The list of founders of all the major dating apps reads like a fraternity roster of Silicon Valley bros, with Whitney Wolfe Herd, founder and CEO of Bumble, currently the major exception.

Why are dating apps entrenched in patriarchal bullshit? You don't have to look much further than their original intention: to keep you playing a game at all costs so their company makes money, so their stock price remains high, and so their shareholders are happy.

In the 2018 documentary *Swiped*, Tinder cofounder and former CSO Jonathan Badeen gleefully confirmed the intentionally addictive element of these dating apps by saying, "We have some of these game-like elements, where you almost feel like you're being rewarded. It kinda works like a slot machine, where you're excited to see who the next person is, or, hopefully, you're excited to see 'did I get the match?' and get that 'It's a Match' screen? It's a nice little rush."

Woof.

Dating-app culture is just a mirror of what's already happening in our male-dominated society, so all the bad (and sometimes illegal) behavior isn't a surprise.

Now, for a bit of devil's advocate. Even though they have many faults, dating apps and online dating in general *can* be a useful tool to meet your person. This chapter is here to help you swipe like the powerful feminist you are, to game the game, take the power back from the toxic tech bros, and use online dating to your advantage.

When I was a matchmaker, I would have to swipe for hundreds of hours on all the apps to find potential dates for my clients. (Seriously, it was the Wild, Wild West out there!) When I did that, I intimately learned the ins and outs of dating apps, uncovered how the algorithms work, and now I'm here to spill all the details. I saw up close how many people are earnestly looking for love online—and not just for hookups (which can also be fun, no judgment). *And* I also saw how dating apps are far from the only answer to finding love.

A study by Pew Research in 2023 said that only 24 percent of lesbian, gay, and bisexual adults and straight adults under thirty met their committed partner online or on an app. Of those adults over thirty and straight, only 10 percent met their partner online. So what's the point of using them if the percentage of "success" is so freaking low across the board?

There are only two reasons to use a dating app—

1. Expanding your social circle, meeting new people, and stretching your connection muscles. Your person could be in the mix (when you use the app with my strategy, of course!).
2. Getting to know your dating personality. This is the most important part. It means knowing what turns you on, what triggers you (and why), how to fiercely ask for your Essence-Based Preferences, and how to set boundaries.

Basically, a dating app is an amazing place to practice being bold as hell with what you want. It can become a place to live out your feminist values without apology. Asking for what you want, out loud and often, with my dating-app strategy leads to more opportunities, more amazing dates, and more agency in your life in general, which can also lead to the right person.

WALKING IN WITH EYES WIDE OPEN

By the time this book is in your hands, the major online dating apps may change, but the vibe will remain the same. This was the topic of the video I made the first time I went viral on social media. I'd been in business for about five years and had just gotten on TikTok. I had about eight hundred followers at the time, then I posted a video about how dating apps are a scam.

With nearly two million views, tens of thousands of new followers, dozens of media requests, and a book deal later, I knew this message was important to share.

Here's the hard truth: with amazing marketing messages, like "Designed to be deleted," swipers have been lured into believing that dating apps are actually working in the interest of helping you find love. But if that were actually true, those dating company shareholders wouldn't be too happy. (All the current major players in the dating-apps arena are publicly traded on the New York Stock Exchange, most via their overlord: Match Group.)

The dirty little secret these companies don't want to tell you is that they're giving you enough of the good stuff to keep you coming back—but not enough of the good stuff to *actually* get you off the dating app with the right person, just like McDonald's fries. But did you know according to *science*, McDonald's fries release dopamine in your brain, the same neurotransmitter that triggers feelings of pleasure? How do they do it? Well, obviously they fry and season them. But they also coat their fries in dextrose, which is a form of sugar. Research has shown that dextrose is addictive as hell, and that's also why I wanted more the minute I was done with a supersize meal.

In a study done by W. Schultz, P. Dayan, and P. R. Montague of the Institute of Physiology in Switzerland, it was found that dopamine release increases according to the predictor of the reward, meaning the matches and messages that the dating app wants you to become addicted to (not to the reward itself, in this dating app case, a great date or relationship).

Basically, this means that your brain starts rewarding you for accumulating matches and messages as the "evidence" that the love you want is happening, which are the reward equivalent to me hoarding McDonald's Happy Meal toys. I thought they made me somehow closer to my ideal self who had all the toys. Why was I so obsessed with those tiny, brittle, off-brand-looking Barbie dolls that came in my Happy Meal? Marketing. Same with dating apps. Their marketing teams have been working overtime to make us all believe these cheap rewards are the answer.

Everyone knows how much dating apps suck. They just don't know what to do about it. So here's exactly how to use dating apps to your advantage.

I also want to offer this additional caveat for women of color—if you're reading this book, I want you to have the extra support you deserve. Because the dating space, especially online, is full of white supremacist, patriarchal bullshit that makes dating objectively harder. And I want you to give yourself all the permission to find love in a way that prioritizes your care and deepens your own liberation.

In the 2021 book *The Dating Divide*, researchers Celeste Vaughan Curington, Jennifer H. Lundquist, and Ken-Hou Lin share, "Many studies have shown a uniquely separate Black experience in online dating, whereby non-Black men and women are least responsive to the messages sent by Black women and Black men." Their research also shows just how prevalent discrimination and male-fetishization is toward Asian and Latinx daters too.

Many of my clients who are women of color have expressed that the online dating experience feels impossible for them. On the one hand, they want to get online to use every tool available to find the right partner, and on the other hand, it's hard to keep going when you get fewer matches and messages and when you're on the receiving end of micro- and macroaggressions, sometimes daily.

This data doesn't mean that you can't find love online with the tools in this chapter (and in this whole book). So many of my clients who are women of color have found love with the mindset and strategy I teach in this book. You deserve to have extra support on your journey to love.

I bring this up because dating online means, in addition to the tools and guidance I give in this chapter, you need to have even fiercer boundaries for yourself and your heart time. You get to prioritize yourself even harder while swiping. You get to call upon your community to support you even more often. It means self-care, self-prioritization, and leaning on your Q/D Questions. Essence-Based Preferences are even more important for your well-being while dating online. Write out your own radical self-care plan. Give yourself permission to have all the boundaries you need to protect your heart. You are not alone, and what you want is completely possible.

Now, let's get into it.

STEP ONE: PICK *ONE* TOOL

You only need to use one dating app because you don't need to waste your time. I hear you yelling in my ear—"But, Lily, what if *every* single person reads your book, follows your advice, and only gets on one dating app? Then I will *never* meet my person because they followed your stinking advice and we were on different apps from each other."

If every single human read this book, the dating world would be a lot more fucking fun and connective and sexy. Plus, I have seen again and again that you will meet your person when you know your EBPs and when you ask for them out loud and often.

The problem is that most of these apps are based on hot, messy scarcity behavior. It comes out on dating apps when you are deep in FOMO (fear of missing out). It's not your fault; dating apps were designed like slot machines, built to keep users pulling that lever in the hope of getting a triple cherry. That kind of behavior leads to swiping on all the apps, getting burned out, deleting them all, and declaring "Never again!"—that is, until you're triggered by your friend who met their new partner on an app and you start the downloading cycle again.

This kind of hot-mess scarcity behavior looks like picking up your phone to check if you got any new matches every ten minutes. It looks like saying yes to matches and messages that you know aren't right for you because you'd rather be talking to someone because you "never know." (But really you do know, they aren't right!)

If the right person for you is on Tinder and you're on Bumble, you will run into them at a coffee shop. Again, it's a tool, not the only answer to meeting your person.

There is also no "perfect dating app." So many of my clients have thoughts like, "I've heard I should be on eHarmony because more serious people are there," or "I should be on the League because they are attracting someone who has a higher degree." I'm so sorry to be the one to break the news to you, but all these "shoulds" are based on really great marketing campaigns. Sure, there might be testimonials to back up the marketing message. But trust me, after swiping on all the apps professionally, I know for a fact that people are people and people are on dating apps.

> **It's time to move like you can't mess this up.**

Choose an app that you like the most (or hate the least). Some factors to consider are: Do you like the user interface design and color scheme? (Seriously, if the color red stresses you out and the minute you see a cartoon flame you get triggered, take that into account and choose a different app.) Dating apps can be such a triggering place to be in general that you want to make this experience as easeful as possible. Your brain will thank you.

Don't pick a niche dating app. Choose one that has a critical mass of users where you are so you can use your limited swiping time to greater success. Don't let your friends who say, "I met my husband on Hinge, so you *have* to be there!" influence you. People meet everywhere, every day. So you might as well spare yourself some cognitive overload in the process and choose the app the feels best to your brain.

My client Catherine had downloaded every dating app ever created. They were mostly gathering dust in a folder tucked away on her iPhone. She would waffle between them, always dipping her toe in each platform until inevitably she would get exhausted and discouraged from the lack of messages and matches.

Her internal story was "If no one wants to be with me on *any* of these dating apps, it must be me, so let me scramble on all of them to prove that story wrong."

It wasn't until we did this work that Catherine realized that she was majorly distracting herself with her dating apps because (a) she was addicted (that's the master plan of an app, after all) and (b) she had a deep fear of ending up alone, so she was spreading herself waaaay too thin. Catherine was punishing herself with all this swiping, and settling was leading to some major dating existential dread.

We did the Dating Detox from chapter 1 and after this intentional break chose *one* dating app for her personality. She was a little freaked ("What if my person is on Tinder and not Bumble?!"). Remember, the right person will make themselves apparent. A dating app isn't the arbiter of your success. But she was finally focusing her energy. And after using this one dating app with my intentional-swiping plan, she started to attract matches and dates that felt aligned with her preferences for the first time.

Decide on one app, then move on.

STEP TWO: WORK FROM YOUR JUICIEST PROFILE PROMPTS

Your dating profile has to be the wittiest, punchiest, better-sound-like-an-*SNL*-writer-wrote-it, most "interesting" 150 characters ever. Otherwise, no relationship for you, sucker.

Just kidding. But if that's what your brain currently believes, we've got to talk.

Between the lines of that mindset is a belief that everyone I've worked with suffers from: "There are so many people here that there's no way I'll stand out, and if I don't stand out I'll never meet someone. And if I never meet someone, then I'm going to die alone a shriveled old maid and my cats will eat my body; it happens. LOOK IT UP."

This thought spiral reminds me of a book I read as a kid, which begins, "If you give a mouse a cookie, he's going to ask for a glass of milk." This little mouse wreaks havoc in his home because this one cookie creates a rabbit hole of needs to fill, and he needs more and more things because he ate the cookie.

The same thing goes for your dating profile. If you start with the belief that you have to "stand out" or "hook someone's attention" by being something or someone other than yourself, you will be diving down the rabbit hole of inauthentic profile prompts, freaking out, and taking anxious actions.

> **What makes your profile magnetic to the right people is *you*.**

Your most essential self, your most passionate self, and your most honest self is what attracts the right people to you. It's not about manipulating your answers to be more interesting. The question really is "How honest can you stand to let yourself be?"

You also don't need to be "chill" in a dating profile. In an episode of the *Las Culturistas* podcast with Bowen Yang and Matt Rogers (#Imareader), guest Jenny Slate said the most brilliant thing on the topic of "chill." She mused that the concept was probably created by a man somewhere who really wanted women to shut up. Hello, misogynist patriarchy!

Let's be real. There's a good chance that if you're reading this book, especially if you have a highlighter and two colored pens, you are not "chill." If you're anything like me, you are intense, strong as hell, have the hottest takes, are a high achiever, and have a zillion things to be proud of. Let's use that intensity to your advantage in your profile.

Side note: This is why I *do not* recommend having your friend group "make over" your dating profile. The committee will always create something that is less essentially you and more essentially them.

Remember your EBPs and your Q/D Questions? They are so gorgeously, essentially you. They are going to make you stand out to the right people for you. So let's use them to fuel your prompts so that they magnetize the right people and repel the rest.

Before downloading the app of your choice, first let's prep your prompts and pics. Open up a Google Doc or pull out a sheet of paper, and let's get to work.

First: Answer your own Q/D Questions. If you chose "What's bringing you joy lately?," answer the question honestly and fully.

Bring some fuck-it energy to your prompts and allow yourself to be fully *you*.

Victoria was stuck on her prompts. She was trying to make them "perfect." Perfectionism is like quicksand. It will submerge you and keep you paralyzed by the "right" next step. Then I asked her to answer my favorite Q/D Question, "What's bringing you joy lately?"

She said, "Women's soccer. But that's boring to talk about in a dating profile."

"Really?" I said. "Tell me what you love about it."

Then she talked for five straight minutes about the players, pay equity, championship games, enjoying games with her family, and traveling around the world to watch these women play.

"Stop," I said. "You have to use this in your profile."

Your joy, your passion, no matter how niche or "weird," will be interesting and contagious to the right people for you. You have to talk about these passions and interests in your dating profile so the right person can be tipped off to your aliveness. It's not that Victoria needed to attract someone who is similarly nuts for women's soccer (though that'd be awesome). It's showing up *yourself* in your dating profile that means the right person can catch on to your joy.

Second: For each of your Q/D answers, circle or bold the big themes that came up. Ask yourself, "What feels specific to *me* and *my* essence?" This is the info you will want to bring into your dating profile prompts.

For Victoria, one of the huge, bolded sections was about women's soccer, travel, and her passion for every inch of that pitch.

Third: Do a Google search on the prompts that are available on that dating app you've chosen. Choose the prompts that allow you to talk about your essence, what brings you joy, what is important to you, and what values you hold and are looking for.

For Victoria, here's how she translated her "what's bringing you joy?" answer to this dating profile prompt:

> **I won't shut up about...** The Washington Spirit. Their championship run, their ownership battle, the awesomeness of women's soccer, and the talent of the players. Looking forward to seeing them in action at Audi field this year with my fam.

Here's what this prompt says to the right person: Victoria is passionate. She is a fan who invests her time, energy, and money into connecting with her passions. She is close with her family. They go to games together. She is up on the drama—especially the ownership battle. She is basically a living episode of *Ted Lasso*. This will be a juicy conversation topic for and with the right person. Talking to people who are passionate is fun, and it can lead to deeper connection.

Another way to create your best dating profile prompt is by using your Q/D Questions. My client Willa also took her EBPs (someone who takes compassionate care of themselves and others, who is passionate about making the world a kinder place, and who is consistent in their communication), matched those preferences with some badass Q/D Questions, and BAM. She put them right in a prompt and answer for her dating profile.

The way to win me over is… by telling me your self-care routine, being consistent in your communication, and sharing what sets your heart on fire!

This dating profile doesn't need to be mega-serious just because it's mega-intentional (unless you are mega-serious and want to share that with potential matches). You get to mix in the high and low of it all. Usually this phrase is talking about something like culture—highbrow would be going to the opera, lowbrow would be watching *Real Housewives*. Both are great and both passions can be inside a person, just like wearing a Gucci belt with an Old Navy T-shirt.

Another client, Tiffany, took the high/low to the next level—sharing her passion for *The Bachelor* and her passion for voting rights in the same sentence. Brilliant.

The sign of a good date is… A conversation that goes to a million places. This could include: our families, the best place for Chinese takeout in DC, the wilderness of *The Bachelor*, and expanding voting rights.

Here's what you don't want, taken from the first draft of my client Lucy's profile.

A trip I took recently… I went to the beach and it was so beautiful. I love being by the ocean!

This said nothing about Lucy's EBPs, except maybe that she travels. Travel is a boring thing to talk about in your dating profile

THE WILD, WILD WEST OF ONLINE DATING

unless you intentionally talk about why travel is important to you, what kinds of trips you take, why, with whom, and what the vibe is on your favorite trips.

Here's the prompt above, with a gorgeous, intentional makeover—

> **A random fact that I love is...** The ocean literally becomes a glowstick throughout the year with bioluminescent plankton; it's stunning and is like the ocean's Aurora Borealis.

This answer says so much about Lucy! It speaks to the fact that when she travels, she values learning new things and gathering unique facts that delight her, especially while away on vacation. See how much more sparkly and specific this answer is than just "I went on a trip"?

Here's an example of how another client, Steph, wove her feminist values into her profile prompts:

> **You should leave a comment if...** You're game for: 1. An American with a slight Southern accent, 2. A little mystical witchy aura (think Stevie Nicks vibes), and 3. Sharing unapologetic feminist values.

The last, super-important piece to your perfect dating profile is explicitly saying what you're looking for. So many women I work with struggle with this. "If I say I'm looking for a relationship, won't that scare people off? Isn't that too serious too quickly? What if I scare off the right person?"

That fear is coming from scarcity and the deep desire to find a partner. There's the assumption that somehow something you say is going to fuck up your chances with the right person. Let me lay this down right here:

> **You can't say the wrong thing to the right person.**

The right person for you is *also* looking for a relationship. So ask for what you want. The downside is that people who are freaked out by you wanting a relationship will disqualify themselves. That's good news. Because they weren't going to be right for you in the first place!

Here are some examples of badass, honest responses to "What are you looking for?"

I'm looking for…

"The right partner to live life fully with, side by side. Then hopefully we go hiking and exploring on six continents!"

"The right partner who is happy spending an afternoon at the Whitney (and lets me read all the plaques) but is also happy to rough it on a backpacking adventure. It's all about the both/and."

"A partner who feels like home everywhere we are. Banter. Meaningful and deep conversations. Adventuring around the world and indulging on the couch."

Let's address an elephant in the room: a lot of people won't read your profile, and that's OK.

There are thousands of dating app users. Many of them swipe and choose only based on pictures, and that sucks.

The point of this gorgeous profile isn't that it will automatically filter out every single human who is wrong for you. *Both/ and* the right people will read your profile. And that's also why you'll create a rock-solid messaging strategy to qualify the right people and disqualify the wrong ones, especially those who are less intentional.

STEP THREE: LOVE ON YOUR PICS

If you felt your nerves spike just now, you're not alone. When I was dating, dating app pictures freaked me out and sent me into an anxiety spiral. "Am I pretty enough? I don't look like those other women, so I won't get matches."

This is the hardest part for my clients. As it relates to your image, being perceived, and your appearance, there can be some thoughts and feelings in the room because your human brain is going to brain. It's going to be comparative because you want to be safe. That's completely normal.

As Chrissy King said in her book, *The Body Liberation Project*, "Here's the reality: You could spend your entire existence worrying about the way your body looks, and you could allow it to cloud your achievements, taint your accomplishments and celebrations, and dull your experiences. But whether it's a pandemic, a chronic illness, a change in lifestyle, birthing a child, or simply the process of aging, all our bodies will continue to change. They were designed to do that. It's inevitable."

Don't let your thoughts about your appearance keep you from allowing yourself to pursue your desires.

If you're finding this part of online dating hard, do this: Notice the negative thoughts you have about your image and your appearance. Instead of toxic positivity–ing your way out of them (which is impossible anyway), name the feeling in your body and practice gentle self-compassion. Gentle self-compassion can sound like, "That's a really hard thought, not a fact, and I'm here with you." Your goal can be to move toward neutrality, if that's available. That could sound like, "It might be possible that the right person will be excited to see me and meet me."

Now, with that out of the way, I firmly believe that you deserve to be captured on camera, right now, as you are right now. You deserve to be seen. So let's get your pics up and running!

Here's the recipe for the best picture lineup for your profile in my recommended order:

- One close-up, happy smile picture (as your first picture in your profile)
- One or two joyful burst pictures
- One full-body picture
- One picture with or doing something you enjoy
- One travel picture
- One or two professional pictures (optional if you love your job)

If you don't have good pictures of yourself, it's time to do something really courageous. Ask a friend to go on a date with you. You're going to bring two or three outfits that you love. Have your friend document your joy throughout the day. I've done a ton of photo shoots in my day, and the secret is this: for every amazing photo, there are between fifty and a hundred meh (or just plain weird-looking) ones. Don't stop trying. Do something that genuinely brings you joy—whether that is brunching with friends, taking a dance class, jumping on a trampoline, or eating cake. Have your bestie take pictures the whole time.

The only two requirements for these photos are:

> **You must be in your joy, authentically.** Don't try to look like anyone else. Go have a ton of fun and have your friend document it along the way.

> **You must be the star of the photo.** It's OK to include a group picture (max three people) if you are obviously the star. This means that you are in the middle and shining bright. This also means you avoid including photos of someone else's star day—your friend's wedding or engagement party, for example.

I think it goes without saying, but don't include photos of kids. If you have kids, you can write about them with your prompts. If the kid is your nephew, niece, or friend's cousin's kid, it's just confusing. Keep your profile just about you.

Validate the hell out of yourself along the way. You're showing up for your desires in all the ways. This is hard and worthy work that will pay off, big-time.

STEP FOUR: SET YOUR BOUNDARIES

I want you to have fewer matches.

Here's what I *don't* want: You have fifteen or fifty messages in your inbox, and when you look at them on a dating app, you want to cry, delete the app, and never look at it again. You have been swiping for three hours and you can't tell who is who anymore. You are overwhelmed, depleted, and burned out, but pushing through.

Fewer matches that are higher-quality means less overwhelm in your dating life. So much of the dating overwhelm, frustration, and anxiety comes from too many options and lack of clarity. What's the right next move? Should I unmatch or give them another chance?

You deserve a really clear set of boundaries in your dating life to protect your heart time.

I define "heart time" as any time you're thinking about dating, talking about dating, or going on a date.

Like a lot of women I know, I had massive trouble setting boundaries in my dating life. I was taught that my needs were not as important as the needs of those around me.

Boundaries, especially in my dating life, had to be grounded in a new belief that was just starting to take root: What if my needs were just as important as someone else's? And what if my needs, being the only ones that I could actually meet, were more important to pay attention to and take action on?

THE WILD, WILD WEST OF ONLINE DATING

What would a dating life look and feel like if you were able to treat your needs and your desires as if they mattered just as much as anybody else's? How would you treat yourself?

Boundaries will allow you to be a badass on a dating app, ruthlessly advocating for yourself and attracting more of the right people (and repelling the wrong ones). Boundaries are as simple as this. Clear is kind and unclear is unkind.

To address cognitive overload, here are the boundaries you need:

No Notifications Needed

You don't need them. A study published in the *International Journal of Environmental Research and Public Health* on "Dating App Use and Wellbeing" in 2023 found that "the number of notifications received can have an effect on users' wellbeing... because high numbers of notifications can lead users to feel overloaded and experience decreased wellbeing, causing fatigue and self-esteem deterioration."

Dating app matches are basically strangers; they don't need (or deserve) your immediate response. Those who do expect an immediate response are addicted to dating apps and it shows. Bless and release.

Hitting Your Swiping Tipping Point

Definition: When you need to put your dating app down for the day.

The right match is not waiting for you to swipe one more minute. If you live your life by that metric, you are going to be exhausted all the time. I recommend about twenty minutes on a dating app per day, swiping and messaging included. Set a timer, then after the timer goes off, put down your dating app for the day. To make this habit stick, do something fun afterward.

Cozy Swiping

Don't swipe on the elevator at work or in bed right before you go to sleep. Intentional effort leads to intentional results. You only need to be searching when you feel awake, cozy, and present (bonus if you're feeling good about yourself a bit or a lot).

I recommend doing five minutes of journaling before swiping—maybe that "Twenty in Two" bragging exercise I showed you in chapter 3.

Cozy swiping also means engaging self-compassion after your swiping session. Don't let frustration, exhaustion, or hopelessness build up without addressing it. Dating apps are hard on everyone's nervous system. So get cozy and engage your self-care majorly after every swiping session.

Bless and Release

You have permission to bless and release anyone at any time for any reason. You don't owe anyone a conversation or your time on an app. Period.

Blessing and releasing can look like unmatching with someone, sending an intentional "I'm not feeling this, wishing you the best" message, breaking up with someone, or blocking their number. Basically, it's protecting your peace without judging yourself.

Here's an incomplete list of people whom I'd recommend immediately blessing and releasing on a dating app:

The Stonewaller. Anyone who doesn't ask you a question back. Don't carry conversations on your back. Asking all the questions in a texting conversation is completely unnecessary emotional labor. Expect the right person to be capable of a back-and-forth conversation.

The Eeyore. Based on the iconic Winnie-the-Pooh character, who when someone said, "Good morning, Eeyore!" once responded with, "If it is a good morning, which I doubt." The Eeyore in a dating app context means you message something like, "What's bringing you joy lately?" and they respond with, "Nothing, everything is terrible." See the rule above. This person is doing their best, bless their heart, but they might need therapy more than a date.

The Most Intense Human You've Ever Met. Basically, this is a person who love-bombs, which according to *Oxford Languages Dictionary* means "the action or practice of lavishing someone with attention or affection, especially in order to influence or manipulate them." They are also way too effusive in their expressions of love or sexual attention. If you feel uneasy or even unsafe emotionally in your conversation, bless and release.

The Pen Pal. This person is not interested in going on a date. They keep talking to you, and maybe the conversation is super sparkly and you feel hopeful about where the connection is going. But if they don't make a move or respond to your move after substantial conversation, they're probably just lonely (or in a relationship) and looking for a text buddy. Bless and release.

You can just unmatch, or, if you want, you can send my favorite bless-and-release message: "Hey! Thanks for chatting. I'm not feeling a romantic connection and wish you the best."

Reaching Your Cutoff Point

Basically, piss or get off the pot. Get decisive and don't waste your time wondering. This is after a certain number of days or messages exchanged, when you either ask someone out or bless and release (or both!).

I generally recommend three to five days of messaging with a maximum of a week and a half of messaging before you either decide that you're going to bless and release or you decide to make an empowered first move.

Making an Empowered First Move

If the person you're chatting with isn't asking you out when you reach your cutoff point, here's what you can do: Cocreate the connection.

This isn't muscling. Muscling would look like asking someone out, confirming the date, planning the date location, making a reservation, confirming plans the day of, and arriving fifteen minutes early. Micromanaging a date in this way comes from a genuine place of wanting something to work. It also reflects a lack of trust that the right person will be able to cocreate a connection or want to do emotional labor to help foster the connection. You deserve someone who is putting in equal effort.

To make an empowered first move, you could say something like, "I've really liked chatting, want to take this IRL?"

If they come back with, "Yeah! Would love to meet up, how's next Tuesday or Wednesday?"

Amazing, they are cocreating.

But if they respond with something murky like, "Yeah, that sounds nice, let me check my calendar," and never get back to you, bless and release.

Unhook from the belief that a match or a message means anything about you or your love-life potential. This is a false metric. Instead, focus on how hard you go for yourself and advocate for your needs, your EBPs, and your boundaries.

HOW TO START THE BEST CONVERSATIONS ONLINE

Open with a Q/D Question that feels best to you. Don't do the unnecessary emotional labor of creating a bespoke message for each person you talk to. When I did that, I was working under the belief that I had to "hook" people in to stand out.

The question "What's bringing you joy lately?" got Mark really excited to answer. Ellie was a client of mine, recently out of an unfulfilling eight-year relationship. She was ready to find someone but was really hesitant to be dating online. With these tools and her plan, she got online and matched with Mark. After she asked this Q/D Question, he responded by talking about his niece (hey, family oriented). Then he asked her the same question in return. Before their first date, they had gone way beneath the surface into some deeper connection. On their first date, he said how refreshing it was to get such a thoughtful question out of the gate. They just got married.

The Q/D Questions are magical openers. They attract the right people and repel everyone else who doesn't want a deeper conversation or connection.

YOU ARE THE CEO OF YOUR DATING LIFE

Fuck my rules. This might sound counterintuitive after this whole chapter but stay with me. I have recommendations based on working with hundreds of humans around the world—and I know that this shit works.

You are also unique. You have your own hot takes and your own experience. This chapter gets to be a cocreation. My expertise meets your self-knowledge. Because at the end of this book, I want you to trust yourself and your gut instincts more than someone else's plan for you.

Try my recommendations as a high-quality experiment. Notice what you need and how your brain responds. I've had clients alter my plan in all sorts of ways based on what their brain and body need. Some swipe for ten minutes a day or download two dating apps. All I care about is that you are setting boundaries and responding to your needs. That is agency.

I don't want you outsourcing the power in your dating life to any coach, author, social media personality, or even your mother or therapist.

It's like being an intern versus a CEO.

The intern looks to her mentor to tell her what to do, where to go, and what to learn. Your mentor might be collaborative, but it's still a relationship based on them knowing more than you, and you needing to learn *their* way of doing things.

The intern asks questions like, "Did I get this right?" or "Why isn't this working?"

These are low-quality questions that imply that the answer is something out there. It also implies that there is something to be "fixed."

When you are the CEO of your love life, you know what you want. The CEO has built incredible things over the years and now there is an area they want to grow. A CEO knows that growth is a prerequisite to their current and future success. They know that growth doesn't mean they've failed or that there is something to fix.

The CEO asks herself high-quality questions like, "What's trying to emerge for me here?" "What skill set do I need to build to get where I want to go?" or "What feels most aligned for me?"

What does the CEO do? She brings on a consultant (someone like me) for this season. I share my hot takes and my next steps, and then you implement and take massive, courageous action.

You now have all the tools you need to date online with badass confidence. Get to it.

MESSY HOMEWORK: Dating Online with Confidence!

1. Decide what online dating resource you want to try with this new approach. There are no wrong answers, and you can always change your mind. Start with the dating site or app you like the best (or hate the least).
2. Use your chosen Q/D Questions from chapter 5 to pick profile prompts on your chosen app.
3. Answer your own profile prompts, using your EBPs and Q/D Questions as inspiration to be fully yourself and to ask for exactly what you're looking for. Remember, you don't have to be the "wittiest" or "chillest." The right person is looking for you to be yourself.
4. Choose pictures that feel most joyful, alive, and most like *you* based on the photo rubric in this chapter.
5. Turn off notifications and declare your cutoff point, bless-and-release message, and swiping-tipping-point boundaries.
6. Choose a start date to reengage your online dating life.
7. Then *start*! Do the "Twenty in Two" exercise from chapter 3 to pump yourself up before swiping.
8. Celebrate yourself! You're doing it! Keep going! You're doing so well. I'm cheering you on as you make all this glorious, messy progress forward. And I know it's creating the joyful-as-fuck dating life you deserve. Let's keep going!

7

Dating In Person with Main Character Energy

This is my favorite part of this book, where I get to remind you about the lost art of in-person dating.

This is where you employ all the courageous-as-hell skills you've been learning. You now will have the opportunity to shake them all up in a gorgeous espresso martini that you will sip poolside in the most stunning silk caftan while feeling unbothered beside an attractive human whom you just asked on a date.

Are you getting the picture? In-person dating requires you to be fully in your Main Character Energy.

Main Character Energy is not a stagnant state of being; it looks different for everyone. It's not like some people have it and some people don't. From coaching hundreds of people, I can tell you it's a learned skill. It's an embodiment. It's taking imperfect action, getting messy, and choosing yourself fiercely.

In-person dating is vulnerable as hell. At least with online dating, you have a screen separating you from another human in an awkward moment. You can put the phone down. With in-person dating, you're getting human smells, sounds, and weirdness, and you're risking rejection. It's super hard. So to combat that hard weirdness, Main Character Energy comes back with one of my favorite Amy Poehler quotes, "You can't look stupid if you're having fun."

At the end of this chapter, not only will you know exactly how to have a juicy in-person dating life, you will be having fun doing it. Asking for what you want, flirting with a cute stranger at a bar, and even making direct eye contact with an attractive stranger on the street can be fun.

So, let's get into it.

Important caveat: For my queer and trans friends reading this, I know that because of the fucked-up world we live in, it might not be physically safe to practice what I am preaching in this chapter. That's why I've included strategies to in-person date that rely on your trusted network instead of dating apps (if you want to take a break from dating online). Take what you need; leave the rest.

In-person dating might feel like the mythical thing that happens to other people, but not you. I hear objections to in-person dating all the time that sound like, "I have *never* been asked out in person. If it hasn't happened by now, it will never happen."

Or, "Wherever I go, there just aren't any people who I want to date or who want to date me. Apps are the only way to meet people nowadays."

Or, "I'm paralyzed by approaching people," so you end up

believing that the other person must make the first move to prove that they're interested. This is a protective mechanism that puts a wall up. It keeps you from opportunities to make an empowered first move that could lead to the love of your life.

As I shared in the last chapter, the truth is that only 10 to 24 percent of singles met their committed partner online in 2023 (based on a 2023 Pew Research study). Meeting an awesome partner in person can happen.

And you don't need an online, protective shield when you have the skill set of Main Character Energy.

THE MINDSET OF MAIN CHARACTER ENERGY

There are three guideposts of Main Character Energy.

First: Give Yourself Permission

If your brain has been serving up thoughts like *In-person dating isn't possible for me. It's never happened before. So why now?*, you need to take a deep breath and a heaping dose of permission.

You have permission to be wrong about what you currently believe is possible. You have permission to not know everything yet. You have permission to try something new.

You have permission to take messy, imperfect action.

Give yourself permission around in-person dating (and honestly anything!) that gets you in the driver's seat of attracting and cocreating the right relationship . It assumes your agency. You can give yourself permission to want what you want, ask someone cute out on a date, bless and release the wrong people with boldness,

THANK YOU, MORE PLEASE

and ask a Q/D Question to a cute human you meet at a party. Even if doing that thing makes you want to shit your pants, you have permission to do both (though hopefully you can skip the poop part).

Giving yourself this kind of expansive permission will get you closer to meeting the right people for you in person. Write yourself a permission slip right now. Maybe it says, "I have permission to learn how to date in person. I have permission to be imperfect at this, and that's OK. I have permission to do bold stuff. My desires are worth it. I have permission to believe that the right person is also looking for me."

Second: Build Self-Trust

Let's be real—you have a great gut instinct. Whether she's loud or soft, she's there. What most people are lacking, especially in their love lives after years of disappointment and false starts, is the skill of acting on that gut.

Maybe you're at a jazz show and the drummer keeps making eye contact with you. You know there's a flirty vibe happening, and a part of your gut says, "Go! Say hi! Give them your number!" But instead, after the show is over, you avoid more eye contact, ask for the check, and run out of there faster than you ever have before.

There are a zillion reasons why you might not acknowledge or act on your gut. Maybe you were taught that you were untrustworthy. Maybe you're healing from trauma and you're just getting back in touch with that little voice inside yourself. In this patriarchal, racist, homophobic, transphobic, and ableist world that we were raised in, you probably were actively told to outsource your trust to someone or something else that held greater power, wisdom, or privilege.

That's why building self-trust is so fucking hard.

Whenever I talk about self-trust in your dating life, I always get some form of, "But, Lily, I trusted myself and I got into a terrible relationship!" or "I've never been in a relationship before. How could I trust myself in my dating life!" Self-trust feels high-stakes for most people I talk to—and that makes sense. You are the only person that you're born with and you die with. You want to trust yourself that you can drive in the right direction. In most of these panicked questions, underneath the surface I hear the assumption that self-trust is all or nothing. Either you have it or you don't. Either you were taught it or you weren't. Either you are or you are not trustworthy. By now, you know how I feel about either/or statements (they suck).

In *Daring Greatly*, Brené Brown describes the act of building trust like this: "Trust is a product of vulnerability that grows over time and requires work, attention, and full engagement. Trust isn't a grand gesture—it's a growing marble collection." I believe the same goes for how you can build self-trust in your love life and your decision-making. It's built in small moments, piece by piece, choice by choice.

Having an instinct, listening to your body, and taking messy, imperfect action is the skill of self-trust. It takes practice to master. But to create a thriving love life, especially in person, you must learn this skill.

One of my favorite thoughts is: *I'm doing the right thing when*

I trust myself. What would your dating life be like if that felt like the truth?

Third: Take Massive Action

This is where you take your permission slip and your growing self-trust, and fuck shit up in a great way. This final step in Main Character Energy means doing the thing. My favorite way to take massive action is with my tool Ten Seconds of Courage.

Approaching someone to say "Hi!," asking someone out, writing your number down on a napkin and passing it to the person you've been flirting with for the last two hours, just takes Ten Seconds of Courage. It's sort of like "Just do it" but with some type A structure.

Taking massive action for your love life will mean getting super vulnerable. It will involve some rejection. With the work you've been doing in this book, you are ready. You have skills to create your own emotional safety, even when things feel out of your control. You get to decide that your desire for connection, for the right partner, is greater than your fear of being rejected, looking dumb, or being judged.

You are resourceful as hell. You learn new skills and figure out things all the time. It's time to move like you can't mess up.

BRING IN YOUR COCONSPIRATORS

The problem: you've not been intentional enough in bringing your loved ones along with you in your dating life. It's not your fault; there's no model or rule book for helping your friends help you. You might look around your friend group, as the only single one, and feel like none of your friends understand you. That can be massively frustrating. So many of my clients share the feeling of being abandoned by their friend group when they're the "only single one left." Dating is so hard that it's like the minute a friend finds a partner, they have selective amnesia and start spewing terrible, discouraging dating advice. They might say things like, "It happened when I least expected it! You should just live your life and it's going to happen." Bless their hearts. No one taught them how to date well either.

> **It's not that your friends are useless in your dating life.**
> **It's that they don't know how to help you yet.**

The people in your life who are your perfect dating coconspirators want to know how to love you better. This process is a concrete way you can teach them how to support you that will actually work.

The theory behind this in-person dating strategy is that both you and your friends' social circles are expanding all the time. They got a new job and have a cute coworker. They went to a work conference and met some interesting folks. They are in a pottery class, and the teacher's cousin comes to your birthday party and BAM! Relationship material appears because your coconspirator is looking out for you. But not just looking around willy-nilly, asking just anyone to go out with you. Coconspiratorship comes with some major structures and rules. What you don't want is to go out on just any date "just because you both are single!" The goal is to help your coconspirator set you up on the best dates of your life.

How the hell do you do that? With your Essence-Based Preferences and your Q/D Questions, of course.

Here's what to do:

Identify Your Ideal Coconspirators

These are people you trust, who don't say problematic stuff about your dating life, and who make you feel safe and seen in your dating life specifically. Make a little list. I recommend starting with one person, and cap it at three people for now. You can totally expand or shrink your list later. They can be single or coupled, just make sure they're someone you really admire and respect.

Be as discerning as Beyoncé choosing her backup dancers. If you know Beyoncé, you know that she only works with the best of the best. She needs the right people on her team, backing her up, and she's not going to give someone a pity invite. You won't find Beyoncé inviting someone because they "should" be on the roster because they were there last year. No, everyone must be working at the top of their game to back up Queen Bey. So it shall be for you and your coconspirators.

Now, what if you have a shortage of incredible, beyond-belief dancers...I mean friends, in your life. What if your friends aren't as supportive as you'd like, or what if you are in a new place without many friends? Let's dispel any of that anxiety right now.

Long-distance friends can still be coconspirators. Supporting you from afar can look like chats about your Essence-Based Preferences, intentional check-ins about your dating life on your regular catch-ups, or chatting after your dates.

You can also use this framework to make new friends who can

then become your coconspirators. For real, you can create EBPs and Q/D Questions to make new friends. You might need more friends anyway—go find them.

Plan the Date

You know when your friend asks you to be a bridesmaid? They ask you to lunch, maybe write you a little card about how much you mean to them, and then ask you to stand with them as they get married? The ritual of bringing on your best friends to support you in a huge life moment can be so meaningful.

Such a special friendship ritual shouldn't be reserved for just a wedding. Asking someone to be your love-life coconspirator is an honor. You are bringing someone in, inviting them into your vulnerable heart time, and allowing them to be a part of your love story. You get to treat this conversation with love and importance.

In this conversation, you'll ask something like, "I'd really like your help in my love life as a connector to new people and as a supporter. Dating can be so tough, and I'd love for you to be my coconspirator to plan and scheme for my dating life, together." Get their buy-in, or if they don't respond positively, move on to another coconspirator option.

Prep Your Boundaries

It's very possible that your friend says something on my "Oh No-No" list. Straight from Tom Haverford's mouth in the classic show *Parks and Recreation*, "Oh No-Nos" are his list of deal-breakers in a romantic relationship ("not loving nineties R & B music" is number three on his Oh No-Nos list). In the case of bringing on your coconspirators, I'm using Oh No-Nos to refer to the things you and your newly minted coconspirator are *not* going to say in the conversation about your love life. These are statements your well-meaning friends and family say that are discouraging as hell. You'll want to avoid these conversational dead ends:

"I JUST DON'T HAVE ANYONE IN MY LIFE WHO I CAN SET YOU UP WITH. I DON'T KNOW WHAT TO DO!"

Oh No-No. We're in this coconspiratorship to develop creative solutions. If you knew other single people, you wouldn't be asking for help. If your friend says this, you can set a boundary. That can sound like, "I want us to come up with creative solutions together. We're both brilliant. So please don't say you're out of ideas. Let's generate some together."

"THERE ARE NO GOOD SINGLE PEOPLE OUT THERE!"

Oh No-No. There are billions of people on this planet. There are infinite ways you could meet someone. If you read that and say, "But, Lily, so many of my friends are amazing women, they are single, and if what you're saying is true, then why wouldn't we all be coupled up by now?"

My response: Couldn't it be true *both* that your friends are amazing and single, that *you* are amazing and single,

> *and* that there are great people out there,

> *and* that any of you could get into the best relationship of your life tomorrow,

and that being single right now just points to the fact
that none of you have settled,

and that might be good news because that means
you will only get into a relationship when it's the
right one for you?!

That's my "both/and" special sauce. It makes everything more
delicious.

"WHY DON'T YOU JUST MOVE?"

Oh No-No. This is implying that both of you are fresh out of
options and that the only next step is to uproot your life for romantic partnership…Not today!

"AREN'T YOU BEING TOO PICKY?"

Oh No-No. Send your friend straight to chapter 4 for this one.
Lowering your standards will not magically bring the right person
to your door. You won't find the right person; you'll just be more
available to the wrong ones.

Look, your friend is a human being. They will say stuff that
isn't the most encouraging sometimes. They have stories, patterns, self-doubt, and patriarchal conditioning just like everyone else. So be aware of their lens. Just because they are in a
relationship does not mean that their opinion or way of going
about dating will work for you. They might say an "Oh No-No,"
and in that case, you get to set a boundary. Remember, teaching
someone how to love you better means asking for what you want
and need. This is practice for asking for what you need in a new

relationship. You might discover that a close friend doesn't have the right mindset or even availability to be your coconspirator. Not everyone is a good fit for your love-life coconspiratorship, and that's OK.

To prepare for any "Oh No-No" moments, it's best to plan this conversation intentionally. And I've found with vulnerable conversations like this one, preparation is the best way to get the most out of this plan. Whenever I know a hard or vulnerable conversation is coming up, I whip out my journal and use the framework in *Radical Alignment* by Alex Jamieson and Bob Gower. I've shared their steps below for you to use at your leisure. In a journal, write out each of these things:

> **Intentions:** Why are you having this conversation? What do you desire here?
>
> **Fears:** In your brain, what's the worst-case scenario? For example, if they say something like, "Oh, you can't find a relationship by yourself? What's wrong with you?"
>
> **Boundaries:** This is your plan when and if an "Oh No-No" happens. For example, you can leave the table, or you can say, "That's not OK with me." It's as simple (and as hard) as that.
>
> **Dreams:** What's the best-case scenario? Maybe they respond *so* well, and with these new tools they have someone in mind immediately for you. Maybe they

make you feel so incredibly seen and held with their response.

Now you're officially ready for this coconspirator hang.

Get Going

On this friend date, after you officially get their buy-in to become your coconspirator, share your EBPs and your Q/D Questions. (There's a cheat sheet at the end of this chapter to help them help you.) You can also give them this book to read with you (book buddies!) so they get the full picture. Basically, whenever they meet someone interesting at work, at an event, or anywhere on their daily travels, they can ask your favorite Q/D Question. If the answer is in line with the vibe you're looking for in your EBPs, they can follow up swiftly with, "Are you single?" Then, BAM! They can make a connection for you.

Inside my program, two clients became friends. (This happens every day. What can I say? My clients are the literal best humans.) They, two badass single women, decided to act as each other's coconspirator. Hannah lived in California, and Sadie lived in Texas. They didn't exactly know how they were going to find dates for each other, but they were open. They shared each other's EBPs and Q/D Questions and were committed to looking out for each other with that mischievous coconspirator twinkle.

Sadie was on a work trip to San Francisco, California, and found herself in the airport on a layover. She struck up a conversation with a dashing guy and found out he lived in San Francisco. Her coconspirator alarm bells were sounding off. She asked him

Hannah's favorite Q/D Question, "I know this is kind of random, but what's bringing you joy lately?" His response: "Oh wow, that's such a good question. Probably my pets. I'm a huge animal lover. And my job, I'm super passionate about what I do." *Ding ding ding!* That was the right vibe (at least at Level 1) for Hannah. So Sadie asked him if he was single. The answer was yes, she got his email address, she downloaded the whole scenario to Hannah, and Hannah and this guy starting dating.

Another client, Addison, asked her close friend to be her coconspirator, and together they came up with a Friday night plan. Every Friday night, they'd go out to a new restaurant or bar to have a great time and make eye contact with cute strangers. After a few weeks, Addison had the courage to approach two cuties and strike up a conversation. Though they didn't lead to dates, these interactions led to Addison's self-concept changing for good. She was completely supported in her love life *and* she was the person who approached cute strangers with ease. This increased her joy and her chances that she would meet someone awesome IRL.

Coconspiratorship is magic. It's cocreation. Being a coconspirator means putting your money where your mouth is and showing up hard for your loved ones and their desires.

This doesn't mean that your coconspirator is the "answer to your dating life." That's just a recipe for pressure and resentment. This is a magical, mischievous cocreation. It's like working at the best, most creative-thinking company. You're heading to the whiteboard together to come up with fun answers to a hard problem. Let's make it more like a playdate with your favorite people.

CREATE YOUR JOY-BUILDING PLAN

Finding the right partner will come when you start having more freaking fun.

In-person dating isn't just "how much people ask you out in the wild." It's how you fill your cup, do things that delight you, and make connections with new people who bring more joy into your life.

Joy building is how I unexpectedly met the love of my life.

I'd moved from the Deep South to San Francisco for a new job. While I was excited to live in a progressive city for the first time in my life, I didn't know a soul. I was super lonely and ready to connect with people. I did something that I'd been super scared of before—I signed up for my first-ever improv class. At the time, I was a hard-core comedy nerd. I would often watch hour-long You-Tube videos of long-form improv sets by performers at the Upright Citizens Brigade theater in New York and LA.

Taking an improv class had always been on my joy wish list of things I would do if I was "feeling brave." I was scared of looking silly, being bad at it, or pooping my pants in class. My brain was serving up no end of worst-case scenarios.

But I was also desperate for real human connection in San Francisco. I was on the bus and my knee touched another human's knee and that level of physical connection made me seriously tear up. In that moment I realized I hadn't so much as hugged another human in a month. It was time for courageous action to create more joy and connection in my new city and new life, so to improv I went.

I found an improv school, paid the entrance fee, and started class. The joy I felt was off the charts. I felt like a kid making friends for the first time. I was playing harder than I had in years. This is where I met amazing, hilarious humans, faced my fears, and met Jessie. She was one of those people who radiated cool and kindness. She was tall, she had glowing red hair, and she was hilarious and full of Midwestern warmth. After class one day, she asked if I wanted to get coffee. I'm pretty sure I turned a deep shade of red and eagerly yelled back, "Um, yeah, that'd be great!" OMG A FRIEND! After our first hang, I knew this new connection had legs.

Turns out, she lived four blocks away from me. So after a few weeks of hanging out after improv class, I'd go over to her house and mooch off her homemade soups and chicken salad for days. It was a golden time.

When I eventually decided to move to New York City, Jessie introduced me to all her close college friends living there. This led to being invited to my first NYC house party, where I met new friends, Phillip and Kate.

Three years later, in June 2017 during a sweltering summer in NYC, I was in that aforementioned toxic relationship and feeling super lonely and out of sorts. Phillip and Kate invited me to their roommate's birthday party. I didn't know their roommate, only that he was an actor and writer named Chris. I just knew that I needed some sort of positive human interaction after the fights I'd been having with my then boyfriend.

I arrived fashionably late (a theme in my life), in a now-famous pink romper from the Gap. My hair was blond with pink streaks and I was ready to party. I was enchanted up to the rooftop by the smell of grilling hot dogs (one of my favorite things) and immediately saw a cute guy in a yellow button-down shirt grilling for his tipsy friends. Turns out, he was the birthday boy.

"Lily, meet Chris. Chris, this is our friend Lily, who we've been telling you about."

The day passed without much fanfare. I had a good time, stayed for at least two plates of delicious food, hugged Chris, said "Happy birthday!," and left. I thought nothing of this first meeting, until July Fourth, just ten days later. I was invited to the same rooftop, and Chris was there. I was wearing the same pink Gap romper. (It was my favorite outfit, OK?!)

Chris and I didn't really interact until I was about to leave. He came over to me and in a slyly casual way, with an air of mischief, said, "I heard you were in a relationship, which is a shame because I wanted to sex you up."

Y'all, this really happened. The man said, "I wanna sex you up," to me. (And for all those who do not get the reference, google it.) I can't lie, his words gave me a little thrill—what I now know as a pussy tingle.

And then I thought, "He thinks he's fucking with me." I couldn't let him get away with something so corny, so obviously trying to get a rise out of me. So without skipping a beat, I said, "I'm in an *open* relationship, so why don't we go downstairs and bang it out right now?"

I saw his brain explode.

He let out a loud, goofy, embarrassed laugh that lasted way too long. It was obvious that he wasn't expecting to be called on his shit by someone he barely knew—especially as his friend was watching the whole interaction unfold from the sidelines, laughing hysterically at his embarrassment.

Then he said, "Ahhh, I'm just kidding. It was fun to see you again. Bye!" And he walked away with all the quickness.

I thought, *Whoa, that was bold, Lily.* And I was proud of myself. Being almost done with a toxic relationship really did amp up my "I don't give a fuck" energy. This is where my Ten Seconds of Courage rule was born.

Two months after that iconic interaction, my toxic open relationship finally ended. I called my friend Jessie, who at that point had also moved from San Francisco to NYC. She invited me over to her home for a hug, charcuterie, wine, and a sleepover. It was exactly the kind of care I needed.

Then my phone buzzed.

It was Chris, texting me. He had found out from our mutual friends that I was newly single, and he made it known that he wanted to get to know me more. I swear to God, at that moment I looked at Jessie and said, "I don't know how I know this, but Chris and I are going to be in a serious relationship…I just feel it."

At that point, I needed some time to heal. In November, when I felt ready to date after my breakup, we went to brunch. It was chilly and Chris held my hands to warm them up. He made me laugh, he asked amazing questions, and I felt this was different. It was a completely joyful date that led to our marriage five years later.

Finding love can be a bonus result of joy building for joy building's sake. Do something that you've always wanted to do, make connections while doing that thing, and then allow those connections to take you to new places and into new relationships.

My joy-building theory for your dating life was confirmed when I read a *Harvard Magazine* article entitled "The Science of Happiness" that said, "Joy, unlike happiness, is not all about me—joy is connection."

Joy building means taking risks. Taking a risk to go to that adult ballet class that would bring you so much joy, but your brain races with, *What will people think of me? I haven't worn a leotard or danced in a decade!*

Wanting to pursue sculpting as your side hustle but hearing your mom in your ear saying, "Who do you think you are? Be more practical!"

Wanting to try a trip to a foreign country you've always wanted to visit, but going alone, your thoughts racing, like, *I always wanted to do this with a partner. What does it mean about me that I'm going by myself?*

Or as simple as you wanting to go to a restaurant in your neighborhood but fearing what people might think if you sit alone.

This is all the same version of this very normal human thought: *I don't want to be rejected.*

That's because rejection literally feels like death. Our bodies are neurobiologically wired to fear rejection like we fear death because when we lived in caves, rejection literally meant being put out into the wilderness to die in the rain. So of course you have this fear. *Both/and* the life you want, that juicy, embodied, rich-as-hell life, is on the other side of pursuing your joy.

Joy gets to become your love-life decision-making standard.

Now, the ability to do things that bring you a ton of joy is a privilege. Not having financial freedom limits your joy-building opportunities for sure.

Both/and no matter where your bank account is, you get to make joy your standard of decision-making in your dating life. Not only because it's more fun, but also because it actually leads to attracting the right people to you.

Now, this isn't that tired, conventional, "Just have fun in your life and the right relationship will come!," basically saying, "Don't pay attention to your dating life; it will all work out!" I believe it will all work out, *and* that you get to take an active role in cocreating that reality.

> **Pursuing your joy is the best dating strategy.**

I've seen again and again that my clients who force themselves out on tons of dates not only are more miserable but also are less likely to feel hopeful and grounded. When feeling hopeless and aimless, these women are more likely to burn out and less likely to meet quality matches. They instead meet a bunch of people who normalize feeling dead across the table.

On the other hand, my clients who are pursuing their joy-building plan are more connected to their bodies, more connected to their intuition and their needs, and more likely to experience hope for their romantic life. They are also more likely to meet people who are in line with what they want and to find the right romantic partner.

I hear you yelling in my ear, "But, Lily, I think a knitting circle would feel joyful and fun, but I don't think anyone I'd be attracted to will be there." I hear this a lot with women who are attracted to men. Unfortunately because of the patriarchal, sexist world we live in, I'm not sure how many men have caught on to the joys of knitting. (And those who have, God bless. You're the change we need to see in the world.)

The point is not to build joy *only* to meet someone romantically. It's to (a) bring more joy into your life and (b) make new connections and maybe even friendships. And (c) the yummy bonus result of this will be more potential romantic connections because you're making more quality, aligned connections in the real world.

Here's what your joy-building plan looks like:

Make a list of at least ten things you could do outside of your house this coming month that would feel joyful.

When you are out in the world doing your joyful thing, your job is to talk to at least one to two people and strike up a conversation. Maybe even start with my favorite Q/D Question, "What's bringing you joy lately?" Make connections. Get messy.

This will feel vulnerable at first. A thought that really helps me with making connections IRL is this: Everyone here is a human and we all desire connection. At the end of the day, we're all still little kids on the playground. And everyone is looking for their kind of people to play with. Give your people that opportunity to find you.

For my introverted friends, I see you. This joy-building stuff might feel incredibly tough, especially when your social batteries are low. Just like everything I teach, you get to make this your own. Maybe you do one joy-building activity per month outside your house. Maybe you bring along two of your coconspirators who act as your wing-women to build connection IRL. Instead of forcing yourself into your vision of what you "should" be doing based on this chapter, ask yourself, "How can I make this work for me?"

Then your job is to take courageous action.

The necessary last step in the joy-building process is celebrating yourself afterward. Celebrating every win, no matter how small, will reinforce to your brain that you're doing something right. After a successful joy-building activity, even if you just said hi to a stranger, even if you were the only one who showed up to the class, it's worthy of a shimmy shake, a dance party, and a celebratory phone call with a friend.

To come up with your joy-building list, ask yourself these questions:

> What out-of-the-house activities feel playful and joyful to me?
>
> What have I always wanted to try that feels a little scary?
>
> What usually stops me from approaching people IRL?
>
> How can I support myself in being courageous next time? (Maybe that means just being a little kinder to yourself or bringing along a friend to encourage you.)

Another version of joy building for your dating life looks like imagining where your ideal person would be having fun, then going to have fun there. Maybe you're looking for a human with amazing friendships who is active and kind of goofy, so you try a low-stakes pickleball league with friends. Maybe you're looking for someone who travels the world to get to know new cultures and who is also passionate about cycling, and you take a group trip to Amsterdam. Maybe you're looking for a Ron Swanson creative type who makes things with their hands, and you try out a wood-working class.

The goal is that this joy-building activity would also bring you joy. It gets you out of your comfort zone and also into that juicy space to envision what your future partner would enjoy.

The Rules of Joy Building

Get in person. Do fun stuff often. Connect with at least one or two new people during each joy-building activity.

Where would your ideal person have a ton of fun? Go have fun there.

Practice Ten Seconds of Courage every joy-building place you go (go up to people; say hello!).

Celebrate yourself after every in-person dating attempt.

Be kind to yourself. This is vulnerable as hell.

In-person dating means taking center stage in your own dang life. It is embodying that juicy Main Character Energy. It's owning what you want and asking for it out loud. Approaching cute people with ease. Taking care of yourself with the utmost compassion. *You* are in charge and capable of creating your most joyful life imaginable. Creating that kind of life will magnetize the right person to you.

MESSY HOMEWORK: A Guide for Your Coconspirator

Here's what to prepare and share with your coconspirator to help them help you. Answer these questions, choose your ideal coconspirator, then plan a friend date to share this plan with them.

1. What do you desire from your dating life right now?
2. How would you ideally like help from your coconspirator for your dating life?
3. What are your top Essence-Based Preferences? Both logistics (on-paper stuff) and, most importantly, the personality traits and values you want.
4. What is *one* Q/D Question you'd like your coconspirator to ask a potential date for you? What does an ideal answer sound like and a "not for me" answer sound like?
5. How can your coconspirator help you get out of your comfort zone, into the real world to build joy and create new connections?

Remember, making messy progress means asking for what you want imperfectly, allowing all your feelings in the process, and taking just one step forward. You've got this!

8

Start Dating, Get Messy

So you've started dating! You have your joyful-as-fuck dating profile and boundaries aligned with your feminist values. You have your in-person dating strategy and coconspirator on board. You're feeling on top of the world and are convinced that this time when you start dating again, it will be different. This book has changed your whole life!

But then you actually start dating and realize some tough shit.

The dating apps haven't changed. There are still the same people there from the last time you burned out. In-person dating still feels awkward and impossible. There seem to be fewer and fewer romantic options for you and the walls feel like they're closing in. Your mom says something like, "Why haven't you brought someone home? Are you even dating?" And the coconspirator you asked to support you hasn't set you up on a date yet.

This is where Heather was. She'd done all the prep work, but then the dating world came crashing down around her. Ghosting, rejection, and exhaustion all led Heather to backslide into old dating patterns (because your brain likes well-worn paths!).

The tools in this chapter are exactly what helped her get unstuck, move into empowered action, and have amazing dates. This chapter is your troubleshooting guide. Flip to it anytime you feel stuck in a pile of dating mud and want to get out.

WHEN YOU GET ON A DATING APP, BUT IT STILL SUCKS

Dating apps are not going to change (I hate this truth, but here we are). The app's job is to be just good enough to keep you coming back, but not good enough to get you matched up well. The good news: The app won't change, but your brain is changing. By engaging your boundaries, knowing your EBPs, and living your feminist values by giving yourself massive permission to want and ask for what you want, you are settle-proofing your love life. Remember, the dating app's job isn't to "prove to you that what you want exists." It's there to be a tool that you are in charge of.

Sure, there will be disappointment. There will be suitors who behave badly or who let you down. Unfortunately and fortunately, we're human. You want something and it's not here yet. That's so tough. So, in light of your humanity, change how you respond to dating apps. Turn toward yourself with compassion. Put your dating app down when you get overwhelmed. Care for your nervous system like your love life depends on it. Ask your bold Q/D

Questions, out loud and often. Notice the stories your brain is telling you based on the app and reframe them swiftly.

Amid the dating app sucking, you might have the thought, *I'm never going to meet someone,* or *This is hopeless.* You might feel panic, dread, and despair about what you want feeling so far away.

Having these thoughts and feelings, while painful, is also very normal. To get unstuck, try the following:

Be More Compassionate with Yourself. Instead of beating yourself up, you can normalize the struggle and turn toward yourself like you would your best friend. Dating apps are activating as hell, and your brain is making it mean that something is wrong. Feeling disempowered really sucks, and this feeling is temporary.

Reframe Your Thoughts to What's Useful and True *Right Now*. For example, you could move your thoughts from *There are no good options here, this is hopeless* and reframe them to *No good matches today, bummer.* Both/and *this silly little app isn't the only way to meet someone awesome,* or *It might be possible that the relationship I want will come, and I get to have my own back.*

A new profile doesn't change a dating app. The new profile gets to be a reflection of the change happening within you, your brain, and your boldness. This will take time to take root.

Having a joyful-as-fuck dating life isn't always immediate. Rewiring your brain's neural pathways and creating a new kind of love life for yourself is an unhurried unfolding.

WHAT TO DO IF YOU AREN'T GETTING ANY DATES

> It doesn't matter if you aren't getting dates all the time.

The number of matches, messages, or dates you go on is not an accurate indicator of how close to or far away from the right relationship you are. Your friend who goes on five dates per week isn't necessarily closer to meeting the right person. She's just more exhausted and has an illusion of control over how quickly she'll meet her person.

Watch the story your brain is telling you about the dates you are or are not getting.

"Playing the odds" in Vegas and going back to that craps table doesn't necessarily mean you're closer to hitting it big. It just means you've lost a bunch of money and have gotten zero sleep because you were glued to the table.

I'm not interested in you having an "illusion of control" over finding the right partner. I want you to have actual control, which means centering your dating life around what you actually have control over. This means defining your Winning Result. This is a concept by coach Simone Seol that I freaking love. It's pursuing the hell out of one thing that you have control over that would have a real impact on your experience of dating.

Simone talks about Winning Results in marketing, and I found her work a few years into running my business (marketing is a scary AF skill to build when you're raised around shitty, bro-y marketing). When I was afraid that I wouldn't make another dollar and no one wanted to work with me (my anxious brain can make up some gnarly stories), I wrote out my Winning Result, the thing I would focus on instead of obsessing over what I couldn't control:

"I will become unafraid of showing up online."

To achieve that Winning Result, I knew I'd be doing stuff I never had before. The first order of business had to be creating safety in my body to do brave shit. That meant taking deep breaths, calming my nervous system with self-compassion, and taking on joyful body movement.

Then I immersed myself in making videos, talking about my program, and showing how I could help people, all the time. It was like immersion therapy. I was terrified at first. But when I focused on winning and celebrating whenever I did something even though fear was present, after a few months of practicing and celebrating myself, I stopped being afraid of being seen. I knew in my bones that I was moving forward in my business and that I was helping people along the way. The bonus was that I attracted the most incredible people into my programs, and my sales were the best they'd ever been.

HERE ARE SOME EXAMPLES OF GREAT WINNING RESULTS FOR YOUR DATING LIFE:

Asking for what you want directly

Blessing and releasing the wrong people swiftly

Celebrating every win (no win is too small)

Asking for support from your coconspirators

Making the dating app mean nothing about you, your future, or your worthiness

Going on dates *only* with people you have intrigue for (instead of settling from the moment you say yes)

Becoming unafraid to approach cute people in person (by doing a lot of it, imperfectly)

The juiciest part of pursuing Winning Results is that Bonus Results are guaranteed to flow from it. Just like if you pursued the Winning Result of eating something green in every meal, you're pretty much guaranteed to poop more regularly (just sharing facts). We're not 100 percent in control of those Bonus Results (like, you don't know exactly how much you'll poop), but you can trust that the bonus will come from showing up hard for what you can control.

Bonus Results for your dating life may include attracting juicy dates, someone awesome asking you out, glowing with confidence, enjoying more micro- and macro-joy in your days, and having less dependence on a dating app. Other bonuses from pursuing the hell out of your dating life might mean that your newfound confidence and "give no fucks" vibe attract an unexpected bonus at work or the clarity and confidence to start your own business. You never know what bonuses will come from pursuing your Winning Result in your love life. Just know the bonuses are also on their way.

With this approach, you will be *winning* from the moment

you start dating. This will lead to more confident and empowered action-taking. So choose your Dating Winning Result now.

To do that, ask yourself: What am I struggling with right now in my dating life?

If you feel behind and hopeless in your dating life, choose the Winning Result "I celebrate every win. No win is too small." Then go collecting wins all over the place and actually plan celebrations for them. Do a shimmy, have a dance party, take yourself out to dinner, and brag to your friends.

If you're obsessing on the dating app, feeling super anxious about your future, and then dress rehearsing tragedy (e.g., "I'm gonna die alone!"), your Winning Result could be practicing the belief "Nothing is wrong. I'm where I need to be."

When your brain is activated during swiping or dating, every time you spiral, sit down for five minutes of self-compassion and then practice a new, useful, and true-feeling thought (in other words, a "baby-step thought") that helps you feel sufficient and safe right now. Here are some options:

> "It might be possible that the best is on its way."

> "It might not be impossible that what I want exists."

> "It might be possible to meet someone amazing."

> "It is safe to want what I want."

This isn't about being a toxic-positivity Polly. You know the type, someone who, in the face of you sharing that you're struggling, yells back, "It's not that bad! You're doing great!" And you're stuck on the other side of the table saying to yourself, "Yeaaaah, that's not helpful."

This is about authentically meeting yourself where you are and figuring out the best, most empowered next step.

Sometimes finding the right dates takes much longer than either of us wants. (I want you to find the most incredible date right *now*, damn it!) The problem is that most people become completely hopeless, give up, and/or outsource their agency to another dating app or dating expert who tells them to change themselves to find love.

Your job in the face of some hard feels of hopelessness is to get in control of what you can and release the rest.

HERE'S HOW TO GET MORE DATES

Choose your Winning Result. Write it down everywhere. Track your progress, and every time you achieve your Winning Result, celebrate the hell out of yourself.

If you haven't been on a date in a while and your brain is freaking out, ask yourself this important question: Are *you* asking anyone out?

"Well, no, Lily, I want them to come to me," or "I put so much effort into taking care of other people, I just want someone else to take the lead of asking me out," or "I don't want to do all the work."

> **Attracting awesome people means making an empowered first move.**

I call it cocreation. Cocreation means showing up to play and seeing if the other person will cocreate a date. It's pitching the date and letting them pick the place. It's showing up, asking for what you want, and then allowing the other person to show up with you.

Think about your favorite friendship. It's probably a beautiful cocreation of texts, hangs, travel, and both of you showing up actively in the relationship. Your romantic life gets to feel this way too.

On the opposite side of never making the first move is muscling. Basically, this is micromanaging your dating life. Asking someone out, planning the date, confirming the time twice, following up immediately afterward, and worrying about the date and what they thought of you.

Muscling is Meredith Grey "pick me" behavior at its worst. If you're not a fan of this iconic *Grey's Anatomy* episode, boy, do you have an epic binge-watching night in front of you. In the scene, Meredith is begging Derek to choose her over his wife (well, kind of ex-wife; it's a classic, gorgeously complicated, Shonda Rhimes–style relationship).

You don't need to beg someone to choose you. You're not in a beauty contest here. You're not stepping up to the mic in a stunning, bejeweled gown, explaining why you, dazzling creature that you are, Miss New Hampshire, are *the* perfect next Miss America.

You're not applying for a job, laying out your credentials to nail the interview and land the position. You do not need to display your qualifications for the role of partner to the right person. Do not ask to be chosen. You get to choose the person who makes you feel how you want to feel (hello, EBPs!) *and* you get to allow them to wholeheartedly choose you too.

When you backslide into "pick me" behavior (which will happen; we're only human), be a loving witness to your brain. Wanting to be chosen is completely normal and human. *Both/ and* it's an act of great power to choose yourself first and allow someone to choose you fully without you needing to convince them.

This is easier said than done. Trusting that someone can choose you is hard, especially if you're used to muscling every connection. In every single romantic relationship I had before my husband, Chris, I was a "pick me" girl. Begging someone to love me and show up for me. In doing that I abandoned myself. It led to a ton of sleepless nights and sobbing phone calls with my close friends.

Here's what I would tell Lily sobbing on her apartment floor ten years ago: You don't need to be chosen by someone else to have value. Being single doesn't mean anything about your value as a person. You inherently have value because you're here, living and breathing on this planet. When the right person comes around, they will choose you so hard that it's undeniable. They will make themselves apparent; you won't have to wonder if they're the right person for you. You'll feel it and they'll show it.

So ask someone out, cocreate a first date, get messy, and bless and release the wrong people. This opens up the time and space for the right people to come in. Make decisions rooted in your self-trust swiftly, practice self-compassion, and keep taking empowered action. To attract amazing dates, double down on your joy-building plan, take on the Dating Bingo card at the end of this chapter, and start marking off squares. This gets to be fun.

WHEN YOU GET REJECTED OR GHOSTED

Whether you liked them a lot or were about to bless and release them yourself, rejection or ghosting is still painful. After being rejected or ghosted, you might be tempted to make up stories about yourself based on ingrained patriarchal conditioning. You might start thinking that you're not "enough" or maybe you're "too much." This is bullshit.

They weren't right for you, and they showed themselves.

You might feel like that person took the power of choice away from you. Take that power back. Their choices show you something very important about them: They are disqualified from your love life. BYE! Time to bless and release them from your heart time.

Despite what your lizard ego brain wants to think, their rejection and ghosting don't mean anything about you. They only mean that you would not have gotten what *you* need from that relationship. It sucks that they didn't think you were right for them, for whatever reason. It's disappointing that they weren't ready for or weren't into a relationship with you.

And they are just one person, among billions of others living on Earth. They are disqualified from your space. Your job is to find someone who actively chooses you so hard that there is no doubt that they're for you.

Before your brain freaks out with thoughts like *What if there's no one who'll choose me?*, take a deep breath. Then allow yourself to reframe that thought with something like *I haven't met everyone yet. I don't know everything. More is possible than I currently realize.*

Now, my friend, if *you* are the one ghosting after a few dates or messages: don't. This is an opportunity to get into the driver's seat of intentionality. Otherwise, you're just jumping out of the car and letting it crash, saying, "It wasn't my fault! I wasn't in there!"

Instead of being like Gary-ghosting-face, use my bless-and-release message for an easy, clear, and kind solution. You can say: "Hi! Thanks for chatting (or going on a date). I'm not feeling a romantic connection, and I wish you the best."

BOOM. Done.

If you backslide into "pick me" behavior, go back to chapter 3, the Brazen Bragging chapter, and remind yourself how awesome you are.

WHEN YOU'RE FEELING WEIRD ABOUT YOUR BODY, YOUR PERSONALITY, OR YOUR FACE

Being a human in this world, much less a woman, is hard as hell. You have to practice self-compassion.

Your brain is an excellent problem solver. But the problem is your brain is looking for *why* you're not in a relationship yet. All the data around you as to *why* probably is skewed. It's so easy to default to "It's because I'm not a certain size, personality type, etc."

The truth is that:

Your body is the right body.

Your face is the right face.

Your brain is the right brain.

The reason it might be hard as hell to believe those thoughts is that the racist, sexist, ableist, fatphobic, transphobic, homophobic, and patriarchal culture has done a great job at convincing us of the opposite. No matter where you are, the work of deprogramming yourself from the cult of not-enoughness is important.

For further study on your inherent worthiness and to dive deep into why your brain is defaulting to hating your body, I recommend building a plan for your liberation by reading these two books: *The Body Is Not an Apology* by Sonya Renee Taylor and *The Body Liberation Project* by Chrissy King.

WHAT TO DO WHEN YOU'RE STUCK IN COMPARISON

There's an episode of *Parks and Recreation* (if you haven't watched every season four times, what have you been doing with your life?) where the character Ann nervously goes to a speed-dating event and sees her coworker Donna. She rushes over to Donna and says, "I am so excited to see you here. These things are horrible when you're by yourself."

Donna shoots her a look and says, "Do you know where you are right now? We're in the jungle. There are no friends here. It's every woman for herself. Dating is a zero-sum game. If you get a man, I don't get that man. Beat it."

In addition to being iconic and hilarious in the show, this moment is a perfect representation of why so many of you stay trapped in a toxic cycle of comparison in dating. In a patriarchal world that values coupled women over single women as "ahead" in life, of course dating would feel like a zero-sum game! Of course it would feel like a competition-filled forest of hustle.

Comparing yourself to other people is normal. You want to belong, and part of belonging in our lizard brains means trying to be like people around you. Dating is so vulnerable, your brain might be reverting to your middle-school-cafeteria self, comparing, scanning, and making sure you're safe.

But comparison won't move you forward. It definitely won't lead to you building a joyful-as-fuck dating life. You don't need to be on the same timeline as your friend to be in the right timing for you. Notice when your brain is deep in comparison mode. Take a deep breath, practice self-compassion, and repeat these thoughts out loud:

"My timing is right for me."

"My love story is and will be unique."

"I have everything I need right now."

"I don't need to know all the steps to be on the right path."

WHEN YOU FEEL TRULY HOPELESS

Feeling hopeless isn't a problem.

Trying to fix that feeling with toxic positivity is the problem.

So many of my clients ask a version of "I feel hopeless, what do I do??????" (All those question marks are literal. The anxiety is real.)

There's nothing wrong with feeling hopeless. It's a feeling, just like excitement, sadness, curiosity, and frustration. They're bodily functions and they're meant to be felt to get to the other side.

The problem is that your brain is making the feeling of hopelessness mean that:

1. You're wasting time feeling this way because you're not feeling confident if you're feeling hopeless;
2. If you're feeling hopeless, you're not putting yourself out there, so then you'll never meet someone and you'll die alone with fifteen cats; so,
3. LILY, SAVE ME FROM FEELING HOPELESS! The panic underneath the surface is a human feeling. But the "must fix this now!" response is sort of like treating your human emotions like a giant pet rat. (No offense to any readers with pet rats...but they are not an animal I want in my personal space. If someone came up to me and was like, "Take my pet rat," I'd be like, "Get that thing away from me!" I'm now a New Yorker, so all I can think of is feral subway rats. Not for me.)

The thought *I feel hopeless and that means I'm behind or wasting my time and will never actually meet someone* is creating the result of spiraling. Making this thought into a fact is actually keeping you stuck. Hopelessness is a feeling, not a fact.

The urge to shove the feeling of hopelessness (or any hard-as-hell feeling) away and instead lean into toxic positivity is like picking at a throbbing pimple all the time and not letting it heal. It sounds like you saying (in a strained, panic-laced voice), "It's not that bad! I just need to get over this! Everything is great!!"

The origin of this toxic positivity pattern is the oily patriarchy. We've all been socialized to mask our true feelings, to be more pleasing, cheerful, and upbeat so as to not disrupt the status quo, to be more accommodating to people (*cough* men) around us. So, a courageous, feminist approach would look like acknowledging your feeling of hopelessness with compassion, feeling the feeling, then taking action to rewrite the neural pathway triggering the feeling in the first place.

I get it, you want something and it's not here yet. The space between those two things can be really painful. Vulnerability means showing up when you can't control the outcome, which is quite literally what you're doing with dating. Not having control sucks. You're gonna have feelings about it.

Feeling your way through your feelings is not only going to give you more access to the depths of your humanness. It's going to give you more access to agency, self-trust, and joy.

Instead of freaking out that you feel hopeless or trying to fix it with toxic positivity, turn toward yourself with kindness. Like my good friend and brilliant feelings expert, Megan Saxelby, says,

"Your feelings are your feelings and you get to have them." You don't have to sit in your feelings forever. Remember, you have to *move* through them to get to the other side. Notice where the sensation is in your body, name the feeling with granularity, take three big deep breaths into that space, and say out loud, "I'm willing to feel anything to be with you." You need to let your body know that no feeling is a deal-breaker to being with yourself. Then keep breathing and noticing the feeling in your body until it rises and passes. This process is magic.

After you honor your big feels and pass through them, it's time to generate the feeling of hope with my Thank You, More Please! Challenge.

THANK YOU, MORE PLEASE!

This is the practice that first sparked the title of this gorgeous book you hold in your hands and is my version of manifesting. It's training your brain to gather evidence that what you want exists *and* that it's closer than you think. Confirmation bias has been getting in the way of seeing the evidence that what you want does exist (and sometimes that it is right in front of you), and this challenge will have you actively looking out in the world for what you want in your dating life and saying, "Thank you, more please!" out loud and often.

This isn't about toxic positivity or forcing your brain to believe what feels impossible right now. It's about slowly exposing your brain to new data that challenges those old stories. Seeing evidence around you that what you want exists sets you up to find it quicker. It sets you up to take more empowered action for your desires.

Here's how to do the Thank You, More Please! Challenge: Keep an eye out for even the tiniest glimmers of what you want in the world. It could be something as small as having a cute, flirty conversation with your barista. Thank you, more please! to cute, flirty interactions! Or you could see a handsome stranger exiting a therapy office. Thank you, more please! to emotional growth and intelligence! It could be an amazing first date with an amazing human, even though you know it won't work with them long term. Thank you, more please! to amazing dates where you have a blast and feel sexy!

When you see a sliver of evidence that what you want exists, say "Thank you, more please!" out loud. It could be whispered under your breath or yelled to the rooftops.

The Thank You, More Please! Challenge doesn't stop there. It's about taking courageous actions too. It's about leaving your number for that attractive waitress or smiling at cute strangers as you walk by on the street. Maybe it's even going into a grocery store, taking out your earphones, and striking up a conversation with someone who catches your eye. Whatever it is, your job is to embrace the challenge and keep saying, "Thank you, more please!" throughout the day.

Here's how this challenge changed my life. I wanted to write this book. I wanted it to be held in your hands like it is right now. I dreamed of the day when my book would be out in the world, being enjoyed by you, my brilliant, gorgeous reader. But a few years back, this dream felt 100 percent impossible. I knew no one who had gotten a book deal. People who got their books published and out into the world felt like they were on Mars and I was on *The Muppet Show*. The opportunity felt so far away that I didn't talk about it out loud. I was afraid I'd look silly to people around me who I assumed also felt like this dream was forever away.

My brain was invested in being right (she's a bit of a know-it-all for the sake of keeping me safe and comfort zoned). She looked for evidence to prove that this opportunity was far away.

But then the desire to share my hot, feminist takes, to help people around the world with a book like this one, grew stronger. The desire could no longer be put on a shelf—she was too loud. I got vulnerable. I went out into the world and searched for evidence that this dream could be possible. I told everyone around me about this dream. Then I was connected to a business coach in the first year of my business. She hosted an event with a book proposal coach, Richelle Fredson, who helps thought leaders get book deals. Thank you, more please! I sat directly to her right, lapping up every word she said. When I had the money a year later, I worked with her. Thank you, more please! Richelle is the reason I got connected to other people like me who'd written a book, and I suddenly was exposed to all this evidence that this book dream was possible. She helped me create clear steps forward to making this dream a reality. Thank you, more please! Two and a half years (and a lot of rejection) later, I got the dreamiest agent and a book deal with the dreamiest publisher.

Putting myself in the way of opportunity and Thank You, More Please-ing evidence that what I wanted existed made the dream feel possible. This led me to taking even bolder action toward my desire.

The Thank You, More Please! Challenge is super *science-y* and based on the Baader-Meinhof phenomenon, also known as the frequency illusion. It's when your awareness of something increases. This leads you to believe the thing is actually happening more, even if it's happening the same amount as it was before your awareness increased. Imagine you grew up in a place where hardly anyone had a red Toyota Prius. Then, one day, you decide you want a red Toyota Prius. Suddenly, you start noticing all these red Toyota Priuses on the road, and you think, *Wait, were these always here? How did I never see them before?* That's precisely what will happen during the Thank You, More Please! Challenge. As you actively look for evidence that what you want exists, your brain will start noticing those moments, and new neural pathways will form. And guess what? That opens up a world of opportunities, both in person and online.

WHEN IT FEELS LIKE YOU'RE MAKING NO FORWARD MOMENTUM IN DATING

Time to bring in some messy, non-perfectionistic, fuck-around energy. What would you do if this was all just play? What if the stakes felt low? What if you couldn't mess up? Who would you text, DM, or ask out? What would you do for fun? What Q/D Question would you ask? Who would you bless and release?

A fuck-around date can also be fun, with the right mindset. When your intention is to bring more pleasure and fun to your dating life, momentum follows. Don't just go on a date that makes you feel yucky or neutral. Go on a date that sounds delightful. Make it your mission to have fun, no matter whom you're with.

Another way to build momentum is to make decisions swiftly. Getting caught up in indecision is a momentum killer. There are probably people who feel iffy on the dating apps or people whom you want to ask out, but you are waiting for them to ask you out so you're in a weird pen pal limbo. Make a decision. At your cutoff point, either ask them out or bless and release. You can't say the wrong thing to the right person. If you feel led to bless and release, you can't bless and release the right person. (If they *are* the right person, they *will* come back into your life.)

Fuck around. Make decisions.

If you're feeling stuck, odds are you have a hard feeling in your body that you've been pushing down for dear life. Notice what's happening in your body and swiftly care for your nervous system. Take three really big deep breaths. Lie flat on the floor and keep breathing. Notice where the feeling is in your body and put compassionate hands on yourself. How can you actually listen to yourself and allow yourself to be human and release any perfectionist fantasies? There's no such thing as being motivated all the time. Don't let those productivity celebrities fool you. Being productive and motivated all the time is not only fake, but also a function of toxic, white supremacist, patriarchal, hustle culture. It's also inextricably linked to capitalism and is harmful to our collective well-being.

THANK YOU, MORE PLEASE

Allowing your timing to be your own is a revolutionary act of self-determination. Giving yourself permission not to be motivated to date all the time is an act of agency. Results aren't linked to how hard you hustle in your dating life. If that were true, you'd be in a relationship already. This is your invitation to pivot toward more ease, honoring your seasons of motivated, excited, and hopeful energy and equally honoring your seasons of rest, hibernation, and healing.

TUNE IN TO YOUR INTUITION AND MAKE EVERY DATE BETTER THAN THE LAST

The answer to the best dates of your life is self-trust.

How do you build dating self-trust? My Date Feedback System.

This tool will help you get out of gut-churning indecision and into deep, clear self-trust.

Before I built the Date Feedback System, I used to bypass self-trust in favor of Did They Like Me Syndrome. Did They Like Me Syndrome equals basing all dating decisions on my perception of whether or not my date liked me. I used this syndrome as a safeguard against rejection. Defining what I wanted based on what another person wanted was a recipe for abandoning myself, which I did in most of my past romantic relationships.

At the same time while I was working as a matchmaker, I had a call with every single client after every single date for feedback. I saw that in hundreds of date feedback calls, almost every single client could intuit whether or not someone was actually interested. Whether or not they acted on their intuition or trusted their instinct was a different story.

I started to realize that self-trust was a superpower. It wasn't that I didn't have self-trust; it was that I was afraid to listen to and act on it.

After my situationships went up in a fiery blaze, I started building a system so I could tune in to my love-life intuition on paper. After all, I knew those relationships weren't exactly right for me at the beginning, but I was too knee-deep in Do They Like Me Syndrome to really notice.

After a date, my brain was swimming in hormones and overwhelmed by all the information my brain was gathering. I would give people too many chances because I felt so confused and overwhelmed about what decision to make. So being super type A, I created a stunning spreadsheet to solve this problem.

After every single date, I would tune in to my intuition, ask myself reflective questions, and hold myself to the standard of honesty on paper. It went well. The more I tuned in, the more I started trusting my gut instincts. The bolder I got, the better my dates got and the more I found people who met my EBPs.

Then I used this process to help my clients get clear on *how* to interpret their intuitive hit after a date and how to act on it. This leads to decisions that direct you to the *right* relationship. It's a superpower that most people leave untapped.

What keeps people from using this superpower and acting on their gut instinct is fear of rejection, exhaustion from all the dating apps, a lack of belief that what they want actually exists, and a lack of clarity on how *they* want to feel on the right date and in the

THANK YOU, MORE PLEASE

right relationship. The Date Feedback System will start sewing self-trust into the fabric of your love life. This will lead to more authentic, vulnerable connections and relationships.

Here's how it works: You're going to create a spreadsheet or grab a notebook that will become your Date Feedback System. After each date you go on, answer these questions within twenty-four hours:

- What was their name?
- How did you meet?
- What did you like about them?
- Was there anything that felt "meh" or just plain bad?
- What did you talk about that made you come alive?
- Did they ask good questions?
- What did you learn about yourself or your preferences on this date?
- What does your intuition tell you about what they felt or thought?
- Do you want to go out again?
- What's the most beautiful and true next step?

Fill in this Date Feedback System within twenty-four hours after every date. This also includes second, third, fourth, fifth dates. This tool will be super helpful in navigating the first few weeks and months of a new relationship.

My client Eleanor was living her best life in Seattle. She had gone on a million dates, most of which were mediocre or just plain bad. She was so overwhelmed in all the bad date muck that

START DATING, GET MESSY

she lost trust that what she wanted was possible. She lost trust in her ability to find the right people.

After going through the work in chapters 1 through 7, she was ready to find the best dates of her life. But it wasn't until using the Date Feedback System that Eleanor finally traded in her self-doubt and criticism for the seedlings of self-trust. With this step-by-step system, she was able to visualize her preferences in a new way, reaffirm what she wanted, and intentionally gather information that what she wanted existed.

The dates she went on kept getting better and better because of her post-date intentionality. Her confidence on and after dates increased. It led to her trusting herself for the first time in her dating life.

WHEN YOU MEET SOMEONE AWESOME

Don't freak out...You have just met someone awesome.

I remember when I went on my first date with Chris, which then led to four dates that same week. I hopped on the phone with a friend the second week we were dating, she asked how it was going, and I replied, "This is really weird. It feels really good, but it's weird."

I was so used to being disappointed, rejected, and ghosted that being in something good felt foreign. At times my brain was fighting against allowing this good thing to come into my life. Gay Hendricks describes this phenomenon in *The Big Leap* as the "Upper Limit Problem." This means that in each area of our lives, there's a perceived cap we have placed on how much career success, wealth, happiness, love, or more we will allow ourselves to have. It's a safety mechanism that keeps you exactly where you currently are so that your brain can control being safe as much as possible. The Upper Limit Problem is usually why you freak the fuck out when the right person or people cross your path.

The way to beat this Upper Limit Problem is to get ahead of it. Prepare to have a moment (or a lot of moments) when you doubt yourself, allow yourself to feel nervous that it won't work out, and create a plan to overcome this Upper Limit Problem.

1. Create calm in your nervous system and safety in your body with breathing deep and practicing self-compassion.
2. Normalize your experience by inviting your closest friends to talk about the new relationship as much as possible without dress rehearsing tragedy. Be in the possibility of this new relationship.
3. Tune in to your EBPs and confirm that this new, amazing human is making you feel how you want to feel in the right relationship. Get brave, share your feelings with this new, amazing human, and ask how they're feeling as well.

Ask for what you want and trust that you can't say the wrong thing to the right person. Hot example coming in. A month into dating Chris, I was yearning for more connection during the week. He would text during the day and evening when he could step away from work, and on the weekends we would have glorious two-day-long dates. But during the week, I wanted more. So I asked him if he'd be open to a phone call each evening with me. He said, "Of course."

Now, you have to know that I love to talk. Like, a lot. Especially with this person I was falling in love with. I would be on the phone for an hour plus every night, talking to Chris, and having the time of my life.

Three months into these hour-long evening chats, Chris said, "I love you, and I think these phone calls are a little long for me. I like to have some unwind time solo each night." So we cocreated a plan to talk for ten to fifteen minutes every evening, instead of an hour. I asked for what I wanted, he asked for what he wanted, and we cocreated a solution together.

Asking questions like, "How do you feel about being exclusive?" or "How are you feeling about our relationship?" or "Can we talk more? I'd love to hear your voice!" is not a deal-breaker or a turnoff to the right person.

This is an excellent example of how getting messy by asking for what you want, instead of playing a perfectionistic game of "how to not say the wrong thing," leads directly to the relationship you want.

I know I said, "Don't freak out!" at the top of this section. But I rescind that. You met an awesome person, freak out. Feel all those feelings. Have a Thank You, More Please! party, yelling it from the rooftops. Allow yourself to trust when something is right. Trust yourself that you will ask the right questions and gather all the information you need along the way to either stay with this person or not. Either way, you get to trust yourself wholeheartedly and have your own back, whether it does or doesn't work out.

WHEN YOU'RE ANXIOUS ABOUT SOMETHING NOT WORKING OUT

Whew, this is a tough one. As a fellow anxious attacher, and someone who will spiral into illogical thoughts in ten seconds flat to protect me from potential danger and rejection, I get you.

Here's what to do when you're spinning out on dating anxiety:

Create an anxiety action plan. This is a one-page list of things you will do when you are feeling anxious. The goal is to move into more emotional groundedness and regulation so you can move forward in your day having your own back. Action steps when you're feeling anxious include:

Move your body. Raise your heart rate with some kind of movement that feels joyful. One of my favorite go-tos is a Beyoncé dance fitness class on YouTube. Even ten minutes helps.

Listen to a self-compassion meditation. My favorites are on Self-Compassion.org (and they're free).

Text your therapist. Set up an appointment. (Or find a great therapist by googling local resources. As of this writing, Psychology today.com is a great place to start.)

Text your bestie. Tell her how you're doing and explicitly ask for support.

Write down your thoughts and be a loving witness to your brain. Then ask yourself, "What else might be true?" or "What's a useful and true thought I can practice about this right now?"

The hard truth is that sometimes we're just anxious—and

maybe that's OK. It's OK to not feel emotionally regulated 100 percent of the time. That's just human. *Both/and* you get to have a plan of action to care for yourself in these moments because you deserve care. Remember, it's safe to be a messy, imperfect human.

If something on this troubleshooting list still isn't helping you get unstuck, here's a magical next step.

GET UNSTUCK WITH HIGH-QUALITY QUESTIONS

High-quality questions are designed to help you get unstuck and into creative problem solving (they're magic everywhere, not just your dating life).

When you have gone on another weird or mediocre date, instead of asking, "What's going wrong?!," take a beat, take a breath, and ask yourself:

"What is trying to emerge here?"

"What am I learning about myself and my preferences?"

"How can I engage in support?"

"What would self-compassion and self-trust say?"

When you engage with these high-quality questions, you are choosing to be creative and brilliant enough to solve your own problems. You are your best solution. I love this advice because it's essentially putting me out of a job, which is *exactly* the point.

I'M GOING TO BELIEVE THIS FOR YOU UNTIL YOU CAN BELIEVE IT FOR YOURSELF

Even with this troubleshooting guide to your dating life, even after doing all this incredible hard and worthy work, sometimes you're going to have those moments. The crying-on-your-bedroom-floor moments. The "Is what I want even possible?" moments.

In 2015 I had one of these moments. I called my friend Rosie, sobbing. She has been my rock in really hard times, and I look up to her like I would a big sister. We navigated the dating world together in my early twenties, and she had just gotten engaged to a great guy. I was equal parts jealous, excited, and mystified as to how she'd met someone who made her so happy.

I was at one of my most hopeless-feeling moments, sitting on my apartment floor. I told her, "I just don't think finding the right person is possible for me. I haven't found anyone close to what I want or how I want to be treated."

Her response: "Lily, this is so painful. There is nothing I can say to make you believe that it's going to happen. But I know in my bones that what is meant for you won't pass you by. That the right relationship is inevitable for you. And I'll believe that for you until you can believe it for yourself."

After going through this process, doing this work, and attracting the love of my life, I can say with complete certainty, she was right. What is meant for you will not pass you by. I'm going to one-up this piece of advice and tell you that I believe that what you desire in your love life is inevitable when you show up and ask for it. I believe this without a shadow of a doubt.

To pass along the legacy of support that Rosie gave me and that a friend gave her before me: I am here in Brooklyn believing that what you want is inevitable in your love life. And I'm going to believe it for you until you can believe it for yourself.

MESSY HOMEWORK: Dating Bingo

Let's make this fun, shall we? Bookmark this page or visit datebrazen.com/bingo to get a printable copy and work to complete all these bingo squares in the next month. Take action, try new things, allow all your feelings in the process, and get messy. And be sure to celebrate every win. Remember, no win is too small. Playing this bingo game will guarantee that you will be dating with more joy and confidence within thirty days.

Make eye contact with 5 cute humans	Take yourself out on a lux date	Say "Hi" to 3 cute strangers	Ask someone out on a date	Set a boundary in your personal life
Do a self-compassion meditation	Take the afternoon off	Have a phone chat with your friend about in-person dating	Ask for what you want directly ALL DAY one day	Approach someone cute and give a compliment
Give yourself permission to do something really silly	Listen to your body OVER your brain	**FREE SPACE**	Let your "just OK" work be enough	"I felt like I was going to throw up and I did it anyway"
Say THANK YOU, MORE PLEASE out loud to 10 things that brought you joy	Go on a date (virtual or in-person)	Bless and release someone	Share your essence-based prefs with your bestie	Celebrate the shit out of yourself
Ask for something audacious	Have a pleasure day—only things that bring you pleasure	Take yourself out on another date	Ask someone on a date	Write a self-compassion letter to your love life

CONCLUSION

My Love Letter for Your Joyful-as-Fuck Love Life

Dear Gorgeous, Brilliant Reader,

Welcome to the end of this book and the beginning of the most epic chapter of your love life. You have done something so brave and revolutionary: you have taken your love into your own hands. You are a badass. You deserve all the champagne pops and dance parties.

Over the last eight chapters, you've done such hard and worthy work. Now it's time to take a deep breath and notice where you've changed. Celebrate the wins you've racked up.

I'm so proud of you, what you've done, the commitment you've made to yourself, and the shedding of shit that doesn't serve you. It's powerful stuff and it will continue to change your life. Thank you for trusting me on this journey. I hope you've realized by now that my aim all along has been to help you trust yourself as the expert.

This process only works if you do the work.

So this is the moment to commit. Commit to being intentional in your love life. Commit to caring for your nervous system and feeling your feelings even harder. Commit to taking messy action, acknowledging every "Thank you, more please" moment when you see evidence that what you want exists, celebrating yourself, and figuring things out with this book when you get stuck.

The one tool you need to move forward is this: worthy action.

Worthy action looks like knowing how to tune in to your own body and feelings. Practicing the belief that you are a safe place to process your emotions. Knowing that you are worthy of taking up space in your own life.

Worthy action looks like *breathing* on dates. It means consistently using your Date Feedback System to keep coming back to self-trust. (I have clients still using it five months into a relationship!) It means believing that you are worthy right now. Not in five pounds, five years, or once you are in a relationship. *Right now.*

As someone who felt like the perpetual last choice for every team, whose every relationship (or date) went up in smoke, I chose to do this work and believe that I was worthy of what I desired. This work led to my freedom. Freedom from the belief that I had to shrink to find love. Freedom from the patriarchal conditioning and perfectionism that kept me stuck. Freedom from any dating advice or rule that didn't serve me. Freedom from centering my wants and desires around whether or not a man wanted to fulfill them.

I hope you learned through this work that you create your own rules. As long as you practice self-trust a little more than you doubt yourself, you will be in your power. You will thrive because you have your own back. You now have the skills to allow the right people in to do life with you.

A year into the pandemic and four years into our relationship, Chris and I decided to get married officially. We'd been living in a tiny Brooklyn apartment together every day, all day, in quarantine for the past year. To us, there was no greater sign that this relationship was right than our daily joy and laughter together. We'd also been wearing rings for years before that (we don't do anything conventionally). Two years into our relationship, I was living in Astoria, Queens, and Chris was visiting for the weekend. We decided to treat ourselves and go to Target. On a whim, Chris suggested that we both wear rings and pretend that we were married for the day. I, of course, jumped at the idea and put on my grandmother's band, which she'd just given me. We walked the aisles of Target, giddy, loudly making jokes about how "my husband is hilarious" and "my wife is so in love with Target." At the checkout line, we bantered with the cashier about the quirks of married life.

We left the store elated that our con wasn't found out. We've worn rings ever since that fateful Target run. Let this be your sign that you are uniquely qualified for the right relationship because, y'all, Chris and I are silly. But I digress.

After deciding to get married officially, we went to a jewelry store and picked out a ring that symbolized our relationship. The minute it came in the mail two weeks later, we stood in our walk-in closet. We had grand plans to go do something New York–y and have a picnic in Central Park with a "down on one knee" moment. But I looked at Chris and said, "I don't want to wait." He said, "I don't either," and he got down on one knee right there, in the closet. He told me how much he loved me, that he wanted to spend the rest of his life with me, and he asked would I marry him. I said, "Yes!" immediately. I started sobbing with joy and felt so much peace. Then I got down on one knee as well and asked him to marry me. Chris teared up, laughed, and said, "Of course."

Two years later, we had the most glorious, unconventional wedding day possible. Our ceremony began by walking toward each other as fifty of our closest loved ones surrounded us in a circle. We greeted all our guests along the way with a hug and so many tears. I didn't hide for one moment of this day. It was my intention to allow, receive, and give myself permission to soak up every ounce of pleasure. I did all those things (messily, imperfectly, just like Chris and I found each other). It was a day full of joy, belonging, and the grounded assurance that this person, this relationship, was the right one for me. It literally changed my brain chemistry.

And even so, my human brain was still a human brain. Along the way toward the wedding, I dress rehearsed tragedy, got super anxious, let it go, got anxious again, and felt excited, nervous, and thrilled all at once. I had to be my own client and practice self-compassion, feel my feelings, and allow frustration when self-compassion felt too slow. Then there was a lot of dancing, therapy, and coaching the hell out of myself with all the softness.

I wish I could say that self-trust meant I had zero anxiety about being in the right relationship; I wish self-trust worked like that with all the good feelings and none of the hard ones. But that's not how being a human works, especially in your love life.

In the months before I got married to Chris, I had a couple of freak-out moments. As an adult child of divorce (or any human thinking critically about the kind of giant, beautiful, and weird commitment you're making), I think it's only natural. A friend of mine heard my fears that sounded like, "What if things change?" and "What if in fifteen years we become different people and want to break up?"

She said, "Lily, your fear of divorce is also rooted in the patriarchy. Just like the thought that a relationship makes you somehow more whole is rooted in the patriarchy. You can trust yourself now and you can trust that you'll trust yourself in five, ten, fifteen, and twenty years too."

Damn, I thought. *She's right.* I realized again how sneaky patriarchal conditioning is. It's constantly trying to crawl up into your joy and your empowered decision-making and make you doubt yourself. This meant that I had more untangling to do, which meant more self-compassion, more feeling my feelings, and more stepping into greater freedom. The right relationship isn't about success or failure; it's about your agency and choice. It's about cocreating something magical and equal and sexy with the right person.

Remember that this work is an unhurried unfolding. The

more you get aware of the patriarchal conditioning, the perfectionism, and the thoughts trying to keep you safe, the more you are invited to deepen your breakthroughs and create new levels of freedom.

You get to trust when something is right for you, just like you get to trust when something is wrong for you. The tools I used to navigate dating joyfully that attracted the best relationship of my life are all rooted in self-trust. The reason you will land in the best relationship of your life is self-trust. Don't get me wrong. This work of building self-trust and listening is hard, vulnerable, and messy as hell. And it's scary because of the perfectionistic narrative that if things change, you were wrong to trust yourself. That's incorrect.

What I realized again then, and every day when I choose self-trust, is that no matter what happens in the next fifty years, I have my own back. When I trust myself, I'm doing the right thing. Period.

Attracting the right relationship, creating emotional safety as you are loved at new levels, and trusting yourself along the way are all possible for you too. Just like they were for Grace.

In 2020, Grace and I worked together. She was a badass, super-successful woman in her mid-thirties, and she hadn't been in many romantic relationships before. She felt perpetually behind in her dating life, which to her made zero sense next to the mountain of things she'd figured out and accomplished professionally. To figure this out, she went through the exact steps I taught you here in this book. The problem was that while she was going through this process, she also was navigating an immense amount of professional stress. Grace had to advocate for herself at every turn to get the most basic respect, and it was exhausting. She was wading through so much bullshit that was out of her control. Building self-trust became even more important.

Grace started learning the skill of self-trust in her dating life, which for her meant taking a break from all active dating for the foreseeable future. She soaked up these lessons, did our Messy Homework, purged her dating life of patriarchal conditioning, asked herself high-quality questions, and allowed herself to rest.

She was a loving witness to the urgent voice in her body saying, "Just start dating! You're wasting your time! Time is ticking away!" She practiced self-compassion and chose instead to believe that her timing was right. She knew that if she trusted herself, she couldn't make the wrong move.

Nine months after Grace and I completed our work, she moved and got a new job, and then this email popped up in my inbox:

> I went on a sparkly first date a month ago, and now it's a full-on relationship?! I can't believe how joyful, safe, boundaried, and fun this feels. He surprised me this morning by showing up at my door at 7 a.m. with my favorite bagel order, so I'd say it's going pretty well. I've surprised myself at so many moments with how I've shown up so far. I'm so much more open, vulnerable, affectionate, communicative, and clear on my needs and wants than I've ever been before. It's felt really freeing

> and made me more secure in the foundation I'm
> hopefully starting to build with this person.
>
> I wouldn't have gotten here without you. Working
> with you truly was like prepping in the off-season
> for what was to come. Who knew? The answer is:
> you did. Thank you, thank you, thank you.

I opened this email and sobbed happy tears. This is it. This is what's possible when you show up for your love life with the right tools and the deepest self-trust. They're still together years later, and their relationship fills me with joy.

This kind of expansive, getting-your-fav-bagel-order-at-7-a.m. kind of relationship is also available for you. I know that in the near future, you will be able to say the same thing: "I didn't think it was possible, but now that I'm in it, of course it was."

Of course what you want is possible.

Of course you get to trust yourself.

Of course your relationship status says nothing about your value.

Of course you get to want what you want.

Of course your love story will be messy, imperfect, and yours.

And of course, the right relationship is inevitable when you show the fuck up for yourself and your desires.

It's not like Grace is different from you. It's not like she's magic and you're not. It's not like I'm magic and you're not. It's the magic of self-trust that is all of ours for the taking. What I want you to take away from this book is the magic of deep confidence in what you want and how to find it.

The joyful-as-fuck dating life and the soul-quenching extraordinary relationship you desire are both on the other side of getting messy and taking aligned, powerful action for yourself and your love life.

Even when Grace was like, "Wait, *how* is this going to work?," she dove deeper into these lessons, took courageous, messy action, and trusted herself along the way. That trust in herself and her desires paid off big-time. And it will for you too.

I'm honored to be your dating coach.

You're ready.

Thank you for showing up for yourself and your love life with me in this book. Now it's time to ask for (and attract) more.

You've got this, and I've got your back.

ACKNOWLEDGMENTS

As someone who reads the acknowledgments section of every book and cries, I'm so pumped it's my turn to thank all the people who made this book possible *(and just fyi, I'm sobbing with joy while writing this listening to* The Holiday *soundtrack so you can join me in this vibe).*

To my literary agent, Johanna Castillo, at Writers House: Thank you for championing me and this book. And thanks also to Victoria Mallorga Hernandez, grateful for all your support.

To my publisher Krishan Trotman: It's an honor to be a Legacy Lit author. Thank you for believing in me and this book. And gratitude to the whole publishing team whose brilliance impacted *Thank You, More Please*—Amina Iro, Elisa Rivlin, Eileen Chetti, Tareth Mitch, Albert Tang, Dana Li, Shreya Gupta, Maya Lewis, and Tara Kennedy.

To my fabulous editor, Leah Lakins: Thank you for every Zoom and encouraging email. Your enthusiasm, support, and expertise helped me get across the finish line with a book I love. Thank you.

To Richelle Fredson, meeting you in February 2020 was one of the best things that has happened to me and my business. Thank you for helping me craft the most beautiful book proposal and for believing everything I wanted was possible. Your friendship means so much to me.

Thanks to my therapist and many awesome coaches along the way. Writing a book is a life excavation and y'all helped me imperfectly, powerfully navigate those waters.

To everyone that has worked on Team Date Brazen the last few years, thank you so much. Especially Jayla Rae. Your support made it possible for me to write a book and run a beautiful business, which is not a small feat. You're the best.

To all my clients, thank you for the endless inspiration. Supporting you and watching you live the lessons inside *Thank You, More Please* has been one of the biggest honors of my life. Thank you also to all my *Date Brazen Podcast* listeners and community. I love being your dating coach.

To Laura Camien and Susan Blackwell: Thank you for helping me slay my creative vampires, move through self-doubt, and start making.

To all my courageous, hilarious, wonderful, inspiring friends: I couldn't have written a book without our rambling walk and talks, text convos, and mutual brag sessions. Megan, Sonia, Jessie, Abby, Rosie, Phillip, Lindsay, Rachel, Damaly, and Martha, thank you. To Chrissy King, thank you for your support and for blazing the author trail before me—you inspire me so much.

To my family: Dad—thank you for teaching me how to write and to write well. Your edits to my fifth-grade papers (and every other paper before and after), while infuriating to me at the time, taught me how to tell my stories, share my heart, and impact people. I love learning from you and am grateful.

Mom—thank you for teaching me how to use my voice. From singing in perfect three-part harmony, to speaking up for myself and others. This skill helps me every day, and I'm grateful.

Hank—your heart, your passion, and your kindness inspire me daily. Thank you for being the most supportive buddy.

Love you all so much.

To my husband, Chris: You are my best-case scenario. Thank you for helping me make this book a reality. For all your love, support, putting delicious food in front of me when I lost track of time writing, coffee talks, and inspiration, I'm immeasurably grateful and lucky. Everything else is just noise.

And to you, dear reader: Thank you for allowing yourself to get support with this book. I hope this sparks a self-trusting, feminist revolution in your love life (and beyond). What you want is possible, and I'll be over here believing it for you until you can believe it for yourself.